OVERTURE OPERA GUIDES

in association with

It is a pleasure to be able to welcome this Overture Opera Guide to Mozart's *Die Zauberflöte* (*The Magic Flute*), the eighteenth to be published since the series in association with ENO was relaunched in 2010.

Mozart's penultimate opera – written in the vernacular, with spoken dialogue and music that ranges from the deeply serious to the light-hearted – has delighted audiences since its premiere in September 1791 at a small theatre tucked away in the Viennese suburbs. Exploring key issues of the Enlightenment, *Die Zauberflöte* is one of Mozart's major contributions to the lyric theatre, and no opera company can be without a production of it for long. This guide's publication coincides with a revival at ENO of director Simon McBurney's staging of the work, a production whose innovative theatricality has won many new admirers for the opera.

I hope that by delving deeper into *Die Zauberflöte*'s background and exploring the many aspects of its score and libretto, readers' appreciation and understanding of this wonderful work will be enhanced.

Daniel Kramer
Artistic Director, ENO
March 2019

The publisher John Calder began the Opera Guides series under the editorship of the late Nicholas John in association with English National Opera in 1980. It ran until 1994 and eventually included forty-eight titles, covering fifty-eight operas. The books in the series were intended to be companions to the works that make up the core of the operatic repertory. They contained articles, illustrations, musical examples and a complete libretto and singing translation of each opera in the series, as well as bibliographies and discographies.

The aim of the present relaunched series is to make available again the guides already published in a redesigned format with new illustrations, many revised and newly commissioned articles, updated reference sections and a literal translation of the libretto that will enable the reader to get closer to the intentions and meaning of the original. New guides of operas not already covered will be published alongside the redesigned ones from the old series.

Gary Kahn
Series Editor

Sponsors of the Overture Opera Guides

for the 2018/19 Season at ENO

Die Zauberflöte

Wolgang Amadeus Mozart

Overture Opera Guides
Series Editor
Gary Kahn

Editorial Consultant
Philip Reed

OVERTURE

OVERTURE OPERA GUIDES
in association with

EN

Overture Publishing
an imprint of

ALMA BOOKS LTD
3 Castle Yard
Richmond
Surrey TW10 6TF
United Kingdom

Articles by Nicholas Till, Julian Rushton and Hugo Shirley first published in
this volume © the authors, 2019

This *Die Zauberflöte* Opera Guide first published by Overture Publishing, an
imprint of Alma Books Ltd, 2019

© Alma Books Ltd, 2019
All rights reserved

Translation of libretto © Kenneth Chalmers

Printed and bound by CPI Group (UK) Ltd, Croydon, CR0 4YY

ISBN: 978-1-84749-805-2

Contents

List of Illustrations

1. Wolfgang Amadeus Mozart, detail from an engraving
by G.A. Sasso after G.B. Bosio, date unknown but
not considered to have been made from life.

2. Emanuel Schikaneder, librettist of *Die Zauberflöte*, director of the Freihaus-Theater auf der Wieden and the first Papageno, engraving by Philipp Richter, *c*.181
3. Reconstruction, now in the Salzburg Mozarteum, of the wooden summer house in the grounds of the Freihaus-Theater which Schikaneder is believed to have lent t Mozart during the composition of *Die Zauberflöte* (below).

4. Playbill for the first performance of *Die Zauberflöte* at the Freihaus-Theater auf der Wieden on 30th September 1791.

5. A Hanswurst theatre in Vienna's Freyung, engraving by Johann Adam
Delsenbach after a 1719 drawing by Emanuel Fischer von Erlach (above).
The role of Papageno is modelled in part on the Hanswurst character.
6. Initiation ceremony at a Masonic Lodge in Vienna, painting by Ignaz
Unterberger in the 1780s (below). Mozart has been variously identified by some
as being seated on the extreme left and by others as on the extreme right.

7. Act One, Scene 3, engraving by Josef and Peter Schaffer, 1795
(above). One of a series of six and the earliest surviving
representations of a staging of *Die Zauberflöte*.
8. Set design for the Act One entrance of the Queen of the
Night by Karl Friedrich Schinkel for the Berlin Court Opera
in 1816, aquatint by C. F. Thiele (below).

9. Set design for the entrance to the temple by Friedrich Christian Beuther for Goethe's production at the Grand Ducal Theatre, Weimar, in 1818 (above).
10. Set design for the temple by Josef Hoffman for the Vienna Court Opera in 1869 (below).

11. Set design for the trials by fire and water by Ludwig Sievert for the Städtische Bühne, Frankfurt am Main, in 1921 (above).
12. Set design for the entrance to the temple by Ewald Dülberg for Otto Klemperer's Kroll Opera, Berlin, in 1929 (below).

13. Jarmila Novotná as Pamina and Alexander Kipnis
as Sarastro in 1941 (above).
14. Joan Carlyle as Pamina and Joan Sutherland
as Queen of the Night in 1962 (below).

15. Fritz Wunderlich as Tamino and Hermann Prey
as Papageno in 1964 (above).
16. Waldemar Kmentt as Tamino and Gundula Janowitz
as Pamina in 1965 (below).

17. Edita Gruberová as Queen of the Night and Elisabeth Speiser as Pamina
in the production co-directed by John Cox and Adrian Slack and designed
by Emanuele Luzzati at the Glyndebourne Festival in 1973 (above).
18. Josef Köstlinger as Tamino with Birgitta Smiding, Kirsten Vaupel
and Britt-Marie Aruhn as the Three Ladies in the 1975 feature
film directed by Ingmar Bergman (below).

19. Leo Goeke as Tamino and Willard White as Speaker in the production
directed by John Cox and designed by David Hockney
at the Glyndebourne Festival in 1978 (above).
20. The lakeside production directed by Jérôme Savary and designed by
Michel Lebois on the floating stage at the Bregenz Festival in 1985 (below).

21. Helen Field as Pamina with the Three Boys in the production
directed by Nicholas Hytner and designed by Bob Crowley
at English National Opera in 1988 (above).
22. Ai-Lan Zhu as Pamina, Gwynne Howell as Sarastro and Howard Haskin
as Monostatos in the production directed by Peter Sellars and designed by
Adrianne Lobel at the Glyndebourne Festival in 1991 (below).

23. Sumi Jo as Queen of the Night in the production directed and designed by William Kentridge at La Monnaie, Brussels, in 2005 (above).

24. Charles Castronovo as Tamino and Albina Shagimuratova as Queen of the Night in the production directed by David McVicar and designed by John Macfarlane at the Royal Opera House in 2013. The production was first seen there in 2003 (below).

25. Maureen McKay as Pamina and Dominik Köninger as Papageno in the
production directed by Barrie Kosky and designed by '1927' (Suzanne Andrade
and Paul Barritt) at the Komische Oper, Berlin, in 2013 (above).
26. Ben Johnson as Tamino and Devon Guthrie as Pamina during the trial by
water in the production directed by Simon McBurney and designed by Michael
Levine at English National Opera in 2013 (below).

27. Pavol Breslik as Tamino and Julia Kleiter as Pamina in the production
directed by Robert Carsen and designed by Michael Levine at the
Opéra Bastille in 2014 (above).
28. The production, set in a schoolroom, directed by Damiano Michieletto and
designed by Paolo Fantin at La Fenice, Venice, in 2015 (below).

29. The killing of the serpent in the production directed by Neil Armfield and
designed by Dale Ferguson at Lyric Opera of Chicago in 2016 (above).
30. Giovanni Salva as Tamino and a bulldozer as serpent in the
production directed by Graham Vick and designed by
Stuart Nunn at the Macerata Festival in 2018 (below).

Die Zauberflöte and the Enlightenment

Nicholas Till

Mozart's last surviving letter, written on 14th October 1791, was to his wife Constanze, who was taking the waters at the spa of Baden, two months before his death.[1] It presents us with a vignette of his routines in the last months of his life. Mozart has been worried about his seven-year old son Karl's schooling (the boy chatters too much, and does nothing but run around in the school garden all day long, as he had unwisely admitted to his father), and he has already made arrangements for Karl to be transferred from his present boarding school in the village of Perchtoldsdorf to the Piarists' school in the Leopoldstadt. He drives out from Vienna to Perchtoldsdorf to collect Karl for a day off school. To the boy's delight – as Mozart reports – he is taken to a performance of his father's most recent opera, *Die Zauberflöte*, which had opened on 30th September at the Freihaus-Theater auf der Wieden. The party includes the composer Antonio Salieri (who afterwards expressed great enthusiasm for the work, describing it as an '*operone*' – a magnificent opera, 'worthy to be performed for the grandest festival and before the greatest monarch'), the singer Catarina Cavalieri, who had performed the role of Konstanze in Mozart's previous German opera *Die Entführung aus dem Serail* in 1782, and Karl's grandmother Cäcilia Weber. After the performance, Mozart drives Salieri and Cavalieri home, then he, Karl and Frau Weber have supper with his sister-in-law Josefa

---

1   Emily Anderson (ed. and trans.), *The Letters of Mozart and His Family*,
     3rd edn. (London: Macmillan Press, 1985), pp. 970–71.

Hofer, Karl's aunt. Finally he takes the boy home where, as Mozart reports, both slept soundly.

This account of a mundane family outing hints at an important aspect of Mozart's last opera. For unlike the venues for his previous works, which had almost all been produced for court operas and aristocratic audiences, Emanuel Schikaneder's Freihaus-Theater auf der Wieden was one of two suburban theatres in Vienna catering for the largely middle-class audience that lived in the expanding outskirts of the city. Like its rival, the Leopoldstadt theatre, it offered a fare of popular entertainment, in German rather than Italian, that combined fairy-tale stories, spectacular sets and knockabout comedy in the tradition of the Viennese Hanswurst drama; it was a genre not unlike British pantomime, with spoken dialogue interspersed with songs and music. It was eminently suitable fare for a family outing, and Karl would surely have been captivated by the tale of heroes and villains, a princess rescued by a prince, *volkstümliche* (popular) music, dancing animals and magical stage transformations.

Mozart used to attend performances of the work regularly during its first run, and in his previous letter to Constanze on 8th October, he had reported on his irritation with a member of the audience who applauded everything 'most heartily', and laughed inappropriately throughout what Mozart describes as 'the solemn scene' at the beginning of Act Two.[2] This is the scene in which Prince Tamino is approved for initiation into the Brotherhood of the Temple of the Sun, from which point the opera takes a decisive new turn as it increasingly references the symbols and initiation rites of eighteenth-century Freemasonry. *Die Zauberflöte* is not only a popular pantomime. It is a symbolic drama with a serious social and spiritual message.

Freemasonry was one of the chief promulgators of the ideals of the Enlightenment in eighteenth-century Europe, spreading from Great Britain throughout the continent during the course of the century. Enlightenment thinking derived from a combination of the scientific enquiry of Isaac Newton and his followers in seventeenth-century Britain and France, and the extreme rationalism introduced

2   Ibid., p. 969.

into philosophical thinking by René Descartes. Everything, it was believed, could be explained by reason and science, which between them offered a fundamental challenge to systems and beliefs based on tradition, authority or superstition. The ideals of the Enlightenment spread throughout Europe via the work of the great French *philosophes* such as Voltaire and Jean-Jacques Rousseau, and were picked up by modernizing, reforming rulers such as Frederick the Great of Prussia and Joseph II of Austria – the latter being described as 'the *philosophe* on the throne' by Mozart's friend Johann Pezzl in his 1783 novel *Faustin*, a copy of which was owned by Mozart.[3] When Joseph assumed power after the death of his more cautious mother Maria Theresia in 1780, he rapidly introduced a whirlwind programme of political, social, economic, cultural and religious reforms that briefly turned the Habsburg empire into the most liberal, tolerant and progressive society in Europe. It was this climate, and the economic boom that it brought about, that in 1781 had encouraged the young Mozart to break away from his hated post in the Archbishop of Salzburg's household to seek his fortune as a freelance composer in Vienna.

In 1784 the prominent Viennese jurist and politician Joseph von Sonnenfels wrote an essay entitled 'On the Influence of Masonry in Civil Society', in which he claimed that Freemasonry had been the chief vehicle for the propagation and dissemination of the Enlightenment in Austria.[4] And indeed, it has been estimated that some eighty per cent of the Austrian higher bureaucracy were Freemasons in the 1780s. The Masonic lodge to which Sonnenfels belonged, and of which he was vice-master, was called 'Zur wahren Eintracht' ('True Harmony'). Its master from 1781 was a scientist, Ignaz von Born, who turned the lodge into the central meeting point of the Viennese Enlightenment. Like any international membership organization, Freemasonry was riven with faction, mainly between the scientific/rationalist and politically progressive strain of Masonry and a more esoteric and mystical strain that harked back to supposedly ancient

---

3   Johann Pezzl, *Faustin, oder das philosophische Jahrhundert* (Vienna: n.p., 1785), p. 332.

4   *Journal für Freymaurer*, (Vienna, 1784), vol. 1, pp. 135–92.

forms of spiritual wisdom. Born had fought vigorously against the growing influence of what he saw as reactionary mysticism in Viennese Masonry, for his dream was to establish an academy of scientific enquiry in Vienna to match the famous Royal Society in London. By 1785 'Zur wahren Eintracht' had 197 members, made up of the intellectual, scientific and artistic elite of the city. The lodge produced a serious scientific journal, and had a significant library. Progressive visitors to Vienna in the early 1780s would invariably head to the lodge to find out what was going on in Enlightenment Austria.

Mozart was closely associated with Sonnenfels, Born and a number of the literary members of 'Zur wahren Eintracht', setting poems by some of the latter to music. In 1785 he wrote a Masonic cantata, *Die Maurerfreude* (K471) in honour of Born. However, although the lodge records tell us that Mozart attended lodge meetings as visitor, he delayed actually joining a lodge until December 1784. And when he did so he did not join 'Zur wahren Eintracht', as we might expect, but a much smaller lodge called 'Zur Wohltätigkeit' ('Beneficence').[5]

My research into the membership of 'Zur Wohltätigkeit' has shown that it was quite specifically the meeting place for those who believed in a *Catholic* Enlightenment in Austria. The idea of a Catholic Enlightenment, let alone Catholic Freemasonry, was, of course, anathema to most Enlightenment thinkers, and Freemasonry itself had been banned by the Pope in 1738. But church reform had been an important part of Joseph II's programme, as it had also of Mozart's hated former employer Archbishop Colloredo of Salzburg. Joseph II, Colloredo and other Catholic reformers in Salzburg and Vienna subscribed to a particular school of reformed Catholicism inspired by the writings of the Italian scholar and theologian Ludovico Muratori. Muratorian Catholicism placed great emphasis upon charity and good deeds, as is reflected in the name of Mozart's lodge: 'Beneficence'. The lodge master was the playwright and literary theorist Otto von Gemmingen, whom Mozart had known in Mannheim in 1777–78, and who edited a

12

moral journal that was dedicated to promoting 'the highest and most righteous feeling for religion'.[6] Mozart, who had been educated in the Muratorian Catholicism that prevailed in Salzburg, clearly hesitated to join 'Zur wahren Eintracht' because, despite his close connections with its members, he could not subscribe to what his pupil Caroline Pichler would later describe as the 'materialist and atheistical' strain represented by the lodge.[7] Instead he waited until a lodge was established that conformed to his own convinced religious ideals.

However, 'Zur Wohltätigkeit' did not survive long as an independent lodge. On 19th December 1785, the thirty or so members of the lodge met with the members of their sister lodge 'Zur wahren Eintracht' to discuss the lodge amalgamations recently commanded by Joseph II. The emperor had grown increasingly suspicious of the secretive activities of the Masonic lodges in Vienna, and in particular the dissemination of the subversive ideas of a group known as the Illuminati, who propounded a much more politically radical agenda than Joseph II, the typical enlightened despot, could accept. The edict gave rise to fierce disputes amongst the Masons themselves, some opposing the decree, others supporting it. Mozart was among the supporters, writing two Masonic songs to commemorate the lodge amalgamations with texts in praise of Joseph's decrees. Those who opposed the decree, mainly members of 'Zur wahren Eintracht', joined the new amalgamated lodge 'Zur Wahrheit' ('Truth'). But 'Zur Wohltätigkeit' was itself now split between those who voted to join with their former sister lodge 'Zur wahren Eintracht' in the new lodge 'Zur Wahrheit', and twenty members, including Mozart, who opted to join the more conservative lodge 'Zur gekrönten Hoffnung' ('Crowned Hope') to form an amalgamated lodge now called 'Zur neugekrönten Hoffnung' ('New-Crowned Hope').

The significance of this meeting and its outcome have been overlooked by historians. But in it were planted the seeds that were to flower in Die Zauberflöte some five years later. For the lodge 'Zur neugekrönten Hoffnung' was well known in Vienna as the centre of a strain

---

6   Otto von Gemmingen, *Der Weltmann* (Vienna, 1782), vol. IV, p.111.
7   Caroline Pichler, *Denkwürdigen aus meinem Leben* (Vienna: n.p., 1844), p. 118.

of esoteric Christian Freemasonry known as Rosicrucianism, to which Mozart was now committing himself. And examination of the symbolism of *Die Zauberflöte* reveals it to be not merely a Masonic opera, as has long been recognized, but more specifically, indeed, a Rosicrucian opera. Hermetic symbols abound in the illustrated frontispiece to the published libretto of *Die Zauberflöte* designed by Mozart's fellow lodge member Ignaz Alberti, and from the arch of the temple there hangs a five-pointed star, an emblem of Rosicrucianism. The opera itself is littered with references to the Rosicrucian number eighteen.[8]

We do not need to trouble ourselves with the tortuous history of Rosicrucianism, adherents to which have included, over the years, Goethe, Debussy and Yeats. For our purposes it is enough to know that late eighteenth-century Rosicrucianism was a form of non-sectarian Christian thinking that drew upon ancient Gnostic traditions, and sought to reunite Christianity under its guidance. Gnosticism posits a radical division between the spiritual and the material, symbolized by light and darkness respectively, and equates materialism with evil. The opening of *Die Zauberflöte* directly references the Gnostic *Hymn of the Pearl* in which a prince from the East[9] arrives in Egypt to seek spiritual wisdom and is first forced to fight with a monstrous serpent (representing materialism), as does Tamino. The name of the high priest of the Temple of the Sun, Sarastro, is clearly derived from the name of the Persian prophet Zoroaster, who taught a dualistic belief system, like Gnosticism. The themes of the spiritual versus the material, of good and evil symbolized by light and darkness, pervade the opera. When Tamino, repulsed from Sarastro's temple, sings, 'O ew'ge Nacht! Wann wirst du schwinden? / Wann wird das Licht mein Auge finden?' ('O endless night! When will you fade away? / When shall I see the light?'), his words are set in the key of A minor, the key furthest

---

8   The Rosicrucian order is the eighteenth degree of one the highest Masonic rites. In the opera, Sarastro makes his first entrance in the eighteenth scene of Act One, there are eighteen seats for the Priests at the beginning of Act Two, the trials of fire and water occur in the eighteenth scene of that act, and so on.

9   The libretto specifies Tamino wearing at his first entrance 'einem prächtigen javonischen Jagdkleide' ('a splendid Javanese hunting costume').

from the opera's central Masonic key of E flat major;[10] the night to which Tamino refers is spiritual rather than merely intellectual.

The real significance of the discovery of Rosicrucian elements in *Die Zauberflöte* is that the revival of Rosicrucianism in the later eighteenth century reintroduced a strain of spirituality into literary and artistic thought that had otherwise been expunged from Enlightenment rationalism. In this respect *Die Zauberflöte* must be seen as a clearly post-Enlightenment work that replaces the Enlightenment's search for rational and scientific understanding of the material outer world with the quest for inner wisdom: 'Aufklärung' (rational enlightenment) is replaced by 'Erleuchtung' (spiritual illumination).

By the end of the 1780s, many writers, artists and thinkers in Vienna had come to distrust the domineering claims of reason and science to be able to explain and command the world. They had also become increasingly alarmed at what they saw as the growing social libertinism that had been brought about by Joseph II's radical reforms at the beginning of the decade. Joseph himself was disappointed and embittered by the failure of his programme, repenting having removed authority from the Church and regretting the subversive effects of the relaxation of censorship. The image of Josephine Vienna was for many people that of a society rife with moral laxity, selfishness, materialism and growing disaffection with its ruler. Like them, the English music historian Charles Burney remembered Vienna in the 'good old days' of Joseph's mother Maria Theresia with affection:

> Her piety has been thought to border on bigotry; but if we may judge of its effect, by the tranquillity, happiness, and affection of her people, compared with the turbulence, discontent, and detestation, of the subjects of her unprincipled, philosophical, and disorganizing successor, we may suppose that too much religion is less mischievous in a sovereign, than too little.[11]

---

10 Among the reasons put forward for the Masonic significance of the use of E flat major is that it contains three flats, which also happen to form the shape of a triangle, the Masonic symbol for the Deity, on the stave.

11 Charles Burney, *Memoirs of the Life and Writings of the Abate Metastasio* (London: G.G. & J. Robinson, 1796), vol. III, p. 253. Punctuation as in the original.

The response of Joseph himself to the growing social laxity and discontent of the Austrian people was to become increasingly repressive and authoritarian. During the latter part of the 1780s, Joseph rescinded many of his liberalizing reforms and established a secret police force, the effects of which were compounded by a serious economic downturn that hit a freelance composer like Mozart particularly hard.

In the enlightened absolutism of Frederick the Great or Joseph II, and in its democratic twin emerging in the Revolution in France, many saw a horrible warning of the dangers of attempting to dictate people's lives by rational and technocratic means alone. Disillusioned with utilitarian social solutions to the problems of human happiness, and horrified by the bloody turn taken by the French Revolution, numerous German thinkers of the period such as Immanuel Kant, Johann Wolfgang von Goethe and Friedrich Schiller turned their backs on political engagement. Instead of seeking material social improvement they urged people to strive for inner freedom. Schiller's words capture this sentiment perfectly:

> In des Herzens heilig stille Räume
> Musst du fliehen aus des Lebens Drang,
> Freiheit ist nur in dem Reich der Träume,
> Und das Schöne blüht nur im Gesang.[12]

Amongst other things *Die Zauberflöte* is, of course, an Orphic parable of the power of art, and more particularly music, to overcome the material forces of nature.

As an aspect of its post-Enlightenment ethos, the opera shares much of its imagery with the poetic allegories of the early German Romantics, in particular the mystical poet Novalis, who wrote two quest and initiation stories which are, like *Die Zauberflöte*,

---

12 Friedrich Schiller, 'Der Antritt des neuen Jahrhunderts', *Sämtliche Werke*, ed. Jochen Golz (Berlin: Aufbau-Verlag, 1980), *Gedichte*, vol. 1, pp. 497–98. 'Into the heart's holy, silent spaces / Must you flee from life's pressures. / Freedom lies in the realm of dreams / And beauty flowers only in song' (present author's translation).

set in a temple of Isis in Egypt, and which tell of the attainment of self-knowledge by the hero. But closer to home, Mozart's friend Johann Baptist von Alxinger wrote a chivalric epic called *Bliomberis*, which appeared in the same year as *Die Zauberflöte*, and tells the story of an Arthurian knight who discovers a secret brotherhood in Africa and, after undergoing some trials of the elements like those undertaken by Tamino and Pamina, gains entrance to the Temple of the Sun. A few years previously Goethe, who is known to have been associated with Rosicrucianism, had written an unfinished poem, *Die Geheimnisse* (published in the Viennese edition of his works in 1789), about a Parsifal-like knight who also applies for admission to a mysterious Christian brotherhood. At its conclusion he hears the sound of a 'mysterious' flute that fills the heart with joy, and sees three boys wearing girdles of intertwining roses (Mozart and Schikaneder's Three Boys in Act Two of *Die Zauberflöte* descend in a chariot bedecked with roses).[13]

This plethora of quest and initiation stories in late eighteenth-century Germany and Austria is indicative of the emergence of the particularly German concept of *Bildung*: self-cultivation based on intellectual and spiritual ideals. The greatest *Bildungsroman* ('*Bildung* novel') is Goethe's *Wilhelm Meister's Apprenticeship*, published 1795–96, in which the young Wilhelm Meister gains self-knowledge through the means of a secret society that is clearly modelled on Freemasonry. But Goethe makes clear that the quasi-Masonic rituals that Wilhelm undergoes are simply 'juggleries and hocus-pocus' to mystify and satisfy the childish curiosity of those whose chief concern is not 'the formation of character' (i.e. *Bildung*).[14] The common sources that fuelled these eighteenth-century literary depictions of initiation, and also the actual rituals of Freemasonry itself, stretch back to the initiation myths and rituals still found in many surviving pre-modern cultures. The American

---

13 Johann W. von Goethe, *The Mysteries* (New York: Mercury Press, 1987), pp. 28–29.

14 Johann W. von Goethe, *Wilhelm Meister*, trans. T. Carlyle (London: Everyman, 1925), vol. II, p. 70.

mythographer Joseph Campbell offered an analysis of the structure of these myths and rituals of initiation, which mark the passage from immaturity to maturity and social integration. This structure can be broken down into two main sections, which tally with the apparently disparate parts of *Die Zauberflöte*. The first part as described by Campbell has five distinct episodes: 1. The call to adventure: the hero is lost in a dark forest or a wild place; 2. The hero refuses the call; 3. Supernatural aid is offered; 4. Crossing of the threshold: the hero meets the custodian and guardian of the threshold. The guardian tests whether the hero is ready for the challenges within; 5. The belly of the whale – or entry into the underworld.[15]

So far it is clear that Act One of *Die Zauberflöte* follows the ancient narrative closely. Tamino, a foreign prince, is lost in a wild and rocky place, where he encounters, and almost succumbs to, a serpent. Having been rescued, he is called by the Queen of the Night and presented with his mission. Although Tamino accepts the challenge, his newly acquired alter ego Papageno refuses, and has to be offered the supernatural aid of the magic bells as talisman (when Tamino also receives the magic flute). Reaching the gates of Sarastro's kingdom, Tamino is confronted by the guardian of the threshold, the Priest, who questions and tests him. At the end of the act, the prince, blindfolded, is allowed admission to the symbolic underworld of the vaults of the temple.

The second section involves the initiation proper. To quote Joseph Campbell:

Beyond the threshold, then, the hero journeys through a world of unfamiliar yet strangely intimate forces, some of which severely threaten him (tests), some of which give magical aid (helpers). When he arrives at the nadir of the mythological round, he undergoes a supreme ordeal and gains his reward. The triumph may be represented as the hero's sexual union with the goddess-mother of the world (sacred marriage), his recognition

---

15 Joseph Campbell, *The Hero with a Thousand Faces* (Princeton: Princeton University Press, 1949), part I, chapter 1.

by the father-creator (father atonement), or his own diviniza-
tion (apotheosis).[16]

Tamino gains versions of all three rewards.

Campbell's reading of this archetypal narrative draws strongly
on Jung, and one aspect of Jung's understanding of the individual's psychic development is clearly relevant to the later Enlightenment's preoccupations concerning the development of the healthy,
integrated individual. But the later Enlightenment and early Romantic writers and philosophers saw this in a broader historical
context, recognizing how modernity itself creates fragmentation
and alienation from the wholeness represented by harmony with
nature (the theme of so much of Rousseau's work). In his account
of the history of humanity in *Über die ästhetische Erziehung des
Menschen* (*On the Aesthetic Education of Man*) of 1795, Schiller
tells of the fall of humankind from wholeness and oneness with
nature, and condemns the shallow reason of Enlightenment culture
(which Mozart and Da Ponte had already satirized in the character
of the 'philosopher' Don Alfonso in *Così fan tutte* in 1789), which
is inadequate to the task of educating humankind. Goethe was also
notably dismissive of one of the more extreme versions of rationalism, the utilitarianism espoused by the English philosopher Jeremy
Bentham, whom Goethe described as an 'ultra-radical idiot'.[17] And
these German writers also saw the French Revolution, the noisiest
historical background to *Die Zauberflöte*, as the clearest indication
of the failings of extreme rationalism: in the *Aesthetic Education*
Schiller warned against attempts to alter society by purely rational
means when people lack sufficient moral and political maturity. In
his play *Don Carlos* (1787), Schiller advanced the view that political
undertakings carried out by rational idealists like the Marquis of
Posa (or Joseph II, or Robespierre) always lead to despotism. Hence
Tamino is first repulsed by voices intoning 'Zurück!' ('Stand back!')
from entering the Temple of the Sun through the Portal of Reason.

16 Ibid., p. 246.
17 Johann W. von Goethe, *Conversations and Encounters*, ed. and trans. David Luke and Robert Pick (London: Oswald Wolff, 1960), p. 275.

Yes, humankind seeks reunification with nature. But understanding of it cannot be obtained through the empirical means of science alone. Thus Goethe's scholar Faust, wearied in his efforts to attain knowledge through rational, instrumental enquiry (the Temple of Reason), rejects science and philosophy in hope of gaining direct access to the Life Spirit itself. Turning to magic, he summons the Spirit of Earth (Nature), who, like the guardians of the Portal of Nature in *Die Zauberflöte*, repulses him: 'And Nature closed to me her sacred doors'.[18] Nature 'scorns an inadequate student', explained Goethe; 'mere empirical intelligence cannot reach her.'[19]

'Men', Schiller writes in the *Aesthetic Education*, 'must fall away from nature by the abuse of reason before they can return to her by the use of reason.'[20] The Egyptian gods Isis and Osiris preside over Sarastro's temple as symbols of Nature and Reason reunited through Wisdom, the final gateway to the temple, which Tamino is not yet ready to enter. But having been accepted for initiation, inside the temple Tamino first undergoes, and passes, the tests of Reason when he is forced to withstand the temptations of the Queen of the Night's Three Ladies, and to resist Pamina and her pleas for acknowledgment of her love. As Tamino withstands the cruel test, Papageno – natural man – says 'Wär' ich lieber in meiner Strohhütte oder im Walde' ('I'd rather be in my straw hut or in the woods'), experiencing what Schiller describes as 'the painful longing to go back home' of those who are alienated from nature, [21] often represented by maternal longing: 'Mir klingt der Mutter Name süße' ('The name of my mother sounds sweet to me') sings Pamina when she tries to explain her desire to escape from Sarastro's kingdom. But there is no route back through regression. Lest we forget the necessity of the biblical expulsion from

---

18 Johann W. von Goethe, *Faust* (I), trans. Philip Wayne (Harmondsworth: Penguin, 1949), p. 89.

19 Johann W. von Goethe, *Conversations and Encounters*, ed. and trans. David Luke and Robert Pick (London: Oswald Wolff, 1960), p. 188.

20 Friedrich Schiller, *Letters on the Aesthetic Education of Man*, ed. and trans. Elizabeth M. Wilkinson and L.A. Willoughby (Oxford: Clarendon Press, 1967), p. 31.

21 Friedrich Schiller, *On the Naive and Sentimental in Literature*, trans. Helen Watanabe-O'Kelly (Manchester: Carcanet Press, 1981), p. 31.

the Garden of Eden as the first step in humankind's path to autonomy, we are reminded by Kant of the angel with the flaming sword who bars man's path back to Eden, which represents 'irresistibly compelling reason', which 'does not allow him to return into that condition of crudity and simplicity out of which it has dragged him'. [22]

The theatre managers of the two suburban theatres, Karl Marinelli at the Leopoldstadt and Mozart's old friend Emanuel Schikaneder at the Theater auf der Wieden, vied with each other to combine the popular Viennese comic tradition with music and spectacle. They ransacked collections of fairy tales and romances to provide vehicles for their theatrical fantasies, and many of these shared sources with Freemasonry, and more particularly the esoteric Freemasonry of Rosicrucianism, whose symbolism in the opera is confirmed as being meaningful by Mozart's previous decision to join a Rosicrucian lodge. Perhaps the most mysterious image associated with the opera is the frontispiece for the libretto, mentioned briefly earlier. The print depicts a temple, and in the foreground, often overlooked, beside the tools of the operative Mason's craft, can be seen the head and shoulders of a dead man. This is Hiram/Adoniram, the murdered builder of Solomon's temple who was the Rosicrucian symbol for Christ, and Mozart himself is three times referred to as Adoniram in the Masonic funeral oration presented at his lodge after his death.[23] Although many of Mozart's contemporaries dismissed Rosicrucianism as occult and mystical nonsense, and it was even condemned as part of a Jesuit plot to regain influence throughout Europe, its aims were, in fact, ecumenical, an ideal expressed in Novalis's essay *Die Christenheit oder Europa* (*Christendom or Europe*) of 1799, which harks back to the spiritual unity of pre-Reformation and pre-Enlightenment Europe, and in Goethe's *Die Geheimnisse*.

22 Immanuel Kant, 'The Conjectural Beginning of the History of Mankind'. Quoted in M. H. Abrams, *Natural Supernaturalism: Tradition and Revolution in Romantic Literature* (Oxford: Oxford University Press, 1971), p. 205.

23 Otto Erich Deutsch, *Mozart: A Documentary Biography*, trans. Erich Blom, Peter Branscombe and Jeremy Noble, 2nd edn. (London: A & C Black, 1966), pp. 447–51.

The post-Enlightenment turn away from social to spiritual concerns in *Die Zauberflöte* means that the opera is not always as apparently socially engaged as some of Mozart's previous operas, in particular in relation to the role of women in society. It is an unfortunate aspect of the dualisms of Western culture that strong women are often cast as figures of malign power, whilst virtuous women are represented as weak and passive. These archetypes are confirmed by a more general misogyny in the opera: when Tamino seeks admission to the temple, saying that an 'unhappy woman' has told him that Sarastro is a tyrant, the Priest reprimands him for listening to women: 'Ein Weib tut wenig, plaudert viel' ('A woman does little, gossips much'); in Act Two the Speaker and the Second Priest warn Tamino and Papageno 'Bewahret euch vor Weiberstücken, / dies ist des Bundes erste Pflicht' ('Beware women's artfulness; / this is the first duty of the Brotherhood'). These are admonitions which clearly reflect some of the less enlightened aspects of Freemasonry itself, which, like many traditional gentlemen's clubs to this day, was an exclusively male environment. As a man of his times, and as a Mason, Mozart could not but share some of these attitudes to women. Yet in the trial scene in *Die Zauberflöte*, in which Tamino must endure the tests of fire and water, he is at the last moment joined by Pamina, who chooses to undertake the trials with him. In this moment the narrative transcends its particular historical conditions to recognize a more archetypal symbolism in which the attainment of spiritual wisdom is achieved through a reconciliation and union of male and female principles. Pamina is not just the prize for Tamino's trial but his necessary partner in the ordeal.

No such reconciliation is offered to Monostatos, the Moor who commands the temple slaves and who has a lascivious passion for Pamina. He eventually joins the Queen in her bid to destroy the temple, and is destroyed with her in turn. Despite being depicted as in some ways pitiable (e.g. his plaint that 'ein Schwarzer hässlich ist... bin ich nicht von Fleisch und Blut' ['a black man is ugly... am I not made of flesh and blood']), his portrayal as exaggeratedly lustful and cruel otherwise identifies him in racist term as the stereotypical non-European Other who threatens the supposedly

superior values of European culture, as the Ottoman Turks in Mozart's day threatened the Habsburg Empire. Such views were prevalent amongst even the most enlightened thinkers of the age such as Immanuel Kant, and were often encouraged in Austria to justify the government's almost permanent military hostilities against the Turks. Schikaneder's and Mozart's (and Kant's) promulgation of this stereotype is regrettable, but we are hardly in a position to judge their views from the perspective of our own society's attitudes to those of different race or creed, and we can only hope that the crown of beauty and wisdom bestowed upon Tamino and Pamina as reward for their love and fortitude brings with it a more tolerant and just vision of society.

* * *

For Mozart, the commission to write an opera for Schikaneder's theatre, by far his most successful opera during his lifetime, opened what could potentially have become a new path in his career. We admire the formal and dramatic perfection of Mozart's Italian operas. But Mozart himself had wanted to establish an authentically German school of opera ever since he had found himself in the German National Theatre in Mannheim in 1777–78. And, if we take his decision to join the lodge 'Zur neugekrönten Hoffnung' as an indication of his intellectual and religious concerns, it was the magical drama of the suburban theatres that provided him with the opportunity to communicate his spiritual ideals to a wider audience. It is perfectly clear that this was his intention with *Die Zauberflöte*. The hybrid form of the suburban *Singspiel*, with its combination of glitzy spectacle and earthy humour, may have seemed an unlikely vehicle for such a serious message. But significantly, *Die Zauberflöte* was highly regarded by Goethe, who held the talent of the opera's librettist Emanuel Schikaneder in high esteem and compared the opera to his own drama *Faust* in its combination of spectacle for the masses and a more profound message for the spiritually aware. Goethe even undertook an (unfinished) sequel to *Die Zauberflöte*. In the contrast between the noble Prince Tamino

and the earthbound Papageno, who is only interested in the bodily pleasures of food, drink and sex (his dream of married life is that of unbridled procreation), we find the nub of the conflict between spiritual and material values. Mozart fervently hoped that his audiences would understand the opera's more profound message. When he took his mother-in-law to the opera, he insisted that she read the libretto first, so that she would understand its message, fearing that she would almost certainly 'see' rather than 'hear' the opera, enjoying its outer theatrical spectacle rather than its inner meanings. 'But what always gives me the most pleasure is the *silent approval*',[24] Mozart had written to Constanze the day before his letter of 8th October 1791 mentioned earlier, and he told her that he had called the overenthusiastic member of the audience who had failed to recognize the work's seriousness a 'Papageno', before changing seats in disgust.[25]

---

24 Anderson, op. cit., p. 967.
25 Ibid, p. 969.

The Music of *Die Zauberflöte*

Julian Rushton

Ist 'Die Zauberflöte' ein Machwerk? This title of a 1978 sympo-
sium poses a question, roughly translated as 'Is *Die Zauberflöte* a
muddle?'[1] If we assume the challenge is directed at the libretto, we
might even answer with a qualified 'yes'; but if it is directed at the
words plus the music, surely the answer should be 'no'. Admittedly,
the stylistic range of the music is extreme, from gravity to comedy, and Mozart's contribution cannot be disentangled from the
words he set. Opera is by its nature a collaboration, and Mozart,
the librettist Emanuel Schikaneder and Schikaneder's troupe at
Vienna's Freihaus-Theater auf der Wieden together created *Die
Zauberflöte*. The previous year the company had presented a no
less fantastical opera, *Der Stein der Weisen* (*The Philosopher's
Stone*), composed mainly by the music director, Johann Baptist
Henneberg, but with contributions from the first Tamino (Benedikt
Schack), the first Sarastro (Franz Xaver Gerl) and also from Mozart;
recently revived, this work proves more than a mere curiosity. *Die
Zauberflöte* itself has needed no such revival, retaining its popu-
larity to the present day because Schikaneder's contribution, and
that of his company's singers, provided the inspiration for some of
Mozart's greatest music.

The first entry of the opera in Mozart's personal catalogue is dated 'In July' [1791]; the music he notated there was not the Overture,
but the Introduction, i.e. the first scene of the opera when Tamino

1   Heinz-Klaus Metzger and Rainer Riehn, *Ist 'Die Zauberflöte' ein Mach-
    werk?*, *Musik-Konzepte*, Nr. 3 (1978).

first appears, pursued by a serpent.[2] Mozart had then to break off
to compose *La clemenza di Tito* for the coronation of Emperor
Leopold II as King of Bohemia; this was his last opera, although
it was performed in Prague two months before the premiere of *Die
Zauberflöte*. A second entry in Mozart's catalogue, dated 28th September, only two days before the *Zauberflöte* premiere, lists two instrumental movements for it, the March of the Priests (opening Act
Two) and the Overture. Unlike the singers' music which would have
needed more time for preparation, these could be quickly rehearsed
before the premiere, and indicate that Mozart had confidence in
the theatre's orchestra to perform his music adequately under such
circumstances. It is also noteworthy that the Freihaus-Theater auf
der Wieden orchestra was as large, at least in the wind sections, as
that of the court theatre where Mozart's other Vienna operas had
been performed.

Overture

Mozart's last overture is among his finest and most complex, and
it introduces elements musically important within the opera itself.
It opens [0a][3] with a theme redolent of nobility and power, but the
following quiet string passage, punctuated by trombones, evokes
mystery. Trombones retain their association with sacred music, in
which they were mainly used at the time. The string rhythm resem-
bles that of the opening fanfare, and of the 'Dreimalige Akkorde',
the massive threefold woodwind and brass chords that punctuate
the Overture and the first scene of Act Two. The following Allegro
is in sonata form. Its main theme – effectively its only theme – is
characterized by repeated notes and a turn [0b]. The idea seems to
have been borrowed from a sonata by Mozart's near-contemporary
Muzio Clementi (in B flat major, op. 24 no. 2), but Mozart's treat-
ment is both more disciplined and more imaginative. It is first ex-
posed as a fugue with four imitative entries, an example of what is

2   The Introduction is so called in the score, as if in French or English rather
    than German, and in Italian ('Introduzione') in the catalogue.
3   Numbers in square brackets refer to the Thematic Guide on pp. 62–66
    [Ed.].

often called 'learned style'; even the first glorious *tutti* continues to deploy this in treble and bass. The secondary material retains the first bar of the fugue subject against decorative counterpoint in the woodwind. The 'Dreimalige Akkorde' divide exposition and development; then Mozart uses another learned device, strict canonic imitation between treble and bass. The return to the opening leads to the recapitulation, where the theme is compressed, prior to a resplendent coda, its full instrumentation anticipating the glowing finale to Act Two. Thus we are prepared for scenes of nobility and grandeur (but also for contrapuntal discipline, notably in the scene with the First and Second Man in Armour who appear in Act Two). Otherwise, however, the Overture hardly prepares us for the alarums of the opening scene, the sufferings of Pamina or the comedy and trials involving Papageno.

Act One

Introduction. Tamino, a prince and unarmed, runs on pursued by a serpent, the tempestuous music no less redolent of terror for being predominantly *piano* [1a, 1b].[4] As he faints, the music is interrupted by the entrance of the Three Ladies who kill the serpent [1c], then turn to look at Tamino. Comedy takes over when they squabble over who should stay with the handsome youth before all going off to tell the Queen of the Night about having found Tamino. This bickering perhaps suggests they are not altogether to be trusted, whereas the other trio of characters we are introduced to in the opera, the Three Boys (sometimes in the past sung by women – less so, however, in recent years), never disagree with each other.

This brings us to the first three solo numbers. First is Papageno, a birdcatcher, who arrives before a revived and wondering Tamino. His entrance [2] adds a new element to the stylistic lexicon. What he sings is not so much an aria as a *song*; here and also in Act Two Mozart gives him repeating (strophic) forms, and a style reminiscent of

4   See Clive McClelland, *Tempesta. Stormy Music in the Eighteenth Century* (Lanham MD: Lexington Books, 2017). On *Die Zauberflöte*, pp. 135–37.

popular music.[5] This characterization through popular song does not mean that Schikaneder, the first Papageno as well as the opera's librettist, was musically limited as a singer: Papageno participates in more complex music at various points later in the opera, including ensembles. Mozart always took advantage of his performers' skills, and would never require anything of them that they could not deliver effectively.

After the clowning of Papageno's mouth being fitted with a padlock by the Three Ladies as punishment for claiming to have killed the serpent, Tamino, alone, contemplates a portrait which the Ladies have given him of Pamina, the daughter of the Queen of the Night. Tamino's gentle aria [3], a meditation on his recognition that he is in love, is through-composed with no repeats. The instrumentation recalls the Countess's aria 'Porgi amor' at the beginning of Act Two of *Le nozze di Figaro*. A flickering violin figure may represent the lover's beating heart – as Mozart said of a similar figure in *Die Entführung aus dem Serail*.[6] The Ladies return and tell Tamino that Pamina has been taken captive by 'ein mächtiger, böser Dämon' ('a powerful, evil demon'). Tamino undertakes to rescue her.

The Ladies then announce the arrival of the Queen of the Night, who enters with music so compelling that we, with Tamino, suppose her trustworthy. This impression is surely helped by the fact that she does not speak any of her words; her scene is all sung. Only in Act Two does she lower herself to speak (to Pamina); and only in the second finale does she join in an ensemble. This first appearance by her has the grandeur of *opera seria*, with the work's first recitative.[7] Schikaneder's printed libretto specifies an 'erschütternder

---

5   The generally performed third verse of this song is not in either Mozart's autograph score or the first printed libretto. It first appears in a printed vocal score as early as 1793, so may well be an addition by Schikaneder following Mozart's death in 1791. It is so indicated in the libretto of this guide, see pp. 76 and 77 [Ed.].

6   Belmonte's aria No. 4 ('O wie ängstlich'). See Mozart's letter to his father of 26th September 1781, Cliff Eisen (ed.), *Mozart: A Life in Letters*, trans. Stewart Spencer (London: Penguin 2006), pp. 435–36.

7   *Die Zauberflöte* has none of the simple recitative of Italian opera, so recitative is orchestrally accompanied throughout.

Akkord mit Musik' ('terrifying chord with music') preceding the Queen's arrival, although, in the event, Mozart didn't actually provide this. He nevertheless composed music for her entry sufficiently alarming for Tamino to tremble, as it again evokes a storm through its syncopations and marked dotted rhythms [4a, 4b]. The recitative is followed by a two-section aria. Through the pathos of the following Andante in G minor [4c], the Queen makes Tamino believe that she truly cares for her daughter.[8] Music may be said not to lie; but, equally, it cannot unequivocally tell the truth, so we do not yet realize that the Queen is recruiting the emotionally vulnerable Tamino for her own nefarious ends. The Andante includes a more majestic middle passage and further expressions of pathos before the final Allegro. Should her subsequent vocal fireworks arouse suspicion? In an eighteenth-century stylistic context, possibly not, although we might equally, and on a similar basis, suspect the integrity of Donna Anna in *Don Giovanni* and of Fiordiligi in *Così fan tutte*, although their passagework is less acrobatic and never reaches the Queen's famous top notes.

The next scene includes the first of two wonderful quintets for the same group of characters and brings Tamino within the comic sphere of the padlocked Papageno [5a]. Later, the quintet touches the sublime. The Three Ladies reappear and sing in turn, as in the Introduction, but here without arguing, and later the first Lady sings solo. With Papageno able to sing words again after his padlock has been removed, all five join in a moral about lying being wrong; but if the words are banal, they are redeemed by Mozart with a bustling Allegro in which the music is closely linked to the developing action. In a transcendent moment, the Ladies praise the magic flute which they give Tamino to help him on his journey to rescue Pamina; more comedy follows when Papageno learns he must accompany Tamino and confront the terrible Sarastro. He is given a set of magic bells; then the men ask for directions. The response is in a slower tempo [5b], with a magical change of instrumental colour: the clarinets, hitherto silent in this number,

---

8 Perhaps significantly, this key reappears in Pamina's aria and twice in the second finale when suicide seems imminent.

replace the oboes. The Ladies explain that three boys will act as their guides.

The scene changes to a 'sumptuous Egyptian room'. Following a conversation between three slaves,[9] music of sung dialogue, typical of *opera buffa*, is used for the Moor Monostatos (at the cadence of which he sounds quite martial) chasing Pamina, whose style is markedly more lyrical than his [6]. Papageno enters, and the action changes from potential rape to farce. This number is nominally a trio, but is really composed dialogue; at the end, the two voices of Monostatos and Papageno briefly sing together (Pamina having fainted) before both run away, each terrified of the other. Papageno returns, to join with Pamina in the exquisite duet 'Bei Männern, welche Liebe fühlen' ('People who can feel love') [7]. Papageno confesses his loneliness, while Pamina has heard from him that Tamino loves her. They are as one, their voices joining after short solos. The music is repeated, except that, as if to show that these two are not social equals, the repeat is decorated by Pamina; she adds more flowing ornamentation (ascending to her highest note) in the coda, 'Mann und Weib, und Weib und Mann, / Reichen an die Götter an' ('Man and woman, and woman and man, / reach towards the divine').

First Finale. What is now marked in the score as finale is an extended section of scenes which runs through to the end of the first act and in which the world of Sarastro and his priests is properly introduced to us. By 1791 Mozart was a past master at extended finales on the pattern established by Lorenzo Da Ponte in the three previous operas of his for which he had provided libretti (*Le nozze di Figaro*, *Don Giovanni* and *Così fan tutte*), usually a single scene with the stage filling until most of the cast are taking part while the music gets faster and faster. The *Die Zauberflöte* finales are different: there is a succession of short separate scenes (five of them for the first-act finale, ten for the second). These both end with choral

---

9   Another, often overlooked, recurrence of the number three throughout the opera (not least in modern productions, which frequently have many more slaves on stage). It is also worth noting that the slaves are not specified as being black in either Mozart's autograph score or in Schikaneder's printed libretto: pointedly, they also refer in their dialogue to Monostatos as 'the Moor' [Ed.].

paeans of praise to Sarastro and his order, and eight of the principal members of the cast do not take part in these closing choruses:
the Queen of the Night, Monostatos, the Three Ladies and the
Three Boys.[10] The first-act finale begins and ends in uncertainty, but
it encompasses the change of perspective within the plot. The second finale begins in near-tragedy before two suicides are forestalled
and virtue triumphs, along with a return to the opera's opening and
principal key, E flat major.

This first finale introduces the Three Boys with extraordinary
solemnity, as they offer advice to Tamino about how to rescue
Pamina. In Mozart's notation, the dotted rhythms [8a] are less se-
vere than the 'Dreimalige Akkorde' or the opening of the Overture,
but the opening chords are for trumpets, trombones and timpani.
Commanding trombone notes (plus clarinets and flutes) punctuate
the Boys' instructions to Tamino, 'sei standhaft, duldsam, und verschwiegen' ('be steadfast, patient and prudent'), as they stress the
severity of the task to be undertaken.

Left alone, Tamino approaches three temple doors. This scene
includes musical elements unlikely to appear in a Da Ponte finale:
recitative and solo song. The music develops into a restless Allegro,
its emotional intensity heightened by long, high notes; neither quite
recitative nor aria, it anticipates the more continuous kind of opera which developed in the following century. When Tamino tries to
enter the first two temples, Mozart provides a descending arpeggio
figure resembling temple scenes in operas by Gluck and, indeed, his
own *Idomeneo*.[11] In an extended dialogue, Tamino seeks, yet seems
to reject, the advice of an elderly Priest (so specified in the score and
libretto, but frequently assigned to the singer of the Speaker), who
tells him that Sarastro is not the demon that Tamino has been led to
believe he is. The Priest concludes by singing with a striking figure –
twice repeated by cellos, and which ties the threads of this extraordinary scene – that Tamino will understand the true situation once he
has been initiated into the Brotherhood. Alone again, Tamino sings
'O ew'ge Nacht' ('O endless night') musically echoing the beginning

10 The Three Boys are on stage at the end of the opera, but not singing.
11 See Gluck, *Alceste* (well known to Mozart), and *Idomeneo*, Act Three.

of the Queen of Night's entrance aria (but in a minor mode) and invisible voices from the chorus, supported by trombones, respond to him with words of hope [8b]. The chorus's second response offers yet more hope by telling Tamino that Pamina is still alive. Tamino's following solo is sung in alternation with him playing his magic flute [8c]. When the opening tune returns, the harmony turns sombre again as he sings, 'Pamina! Höre mich! Umsonst!' ('Pamina! Hear me! In vain!'), then his upward scale is echoed by Papageno's pipes. Comedy follows as Tamino leaves the stage and Papageno enters with Pamina from the other side. Monostatos, in pursuit, mockingly picks up their musical motif and the stage fills as the tempo quickens. Slaves bind the escaping pair, but Papageno remembers his magic bells, and to an ethereal texture – glockenspiel and pizzicato strings – the slaves and Monostatos dance away, entranced. Pamina and Papageno, here singing as equals, praise the soothing effect of the bells to a delicious folk-like tune.

A fanfare of trumpets prepares the entry of Sarastro and offers Papageno another chance to register abject fear. Pamina, however, resolves to tell the truth (*Wahrheit*) 'even though it be a crime':

The martial style of the fanfare resumes with choral praise of Sarastro, and the stage fills with priests and attendants. Pamina in measured declamation confesses to Sarastro her wish to escape for fear of Monostatos. Finally, we hear from Sarastro himself telling Pamina that he knows she 'loves another deeply', at which point the music becomes more lyrical.

Near the end of this fine, orotund passage, Sarastro shows off the solemn low notes that contrast with the extreme high notes of the Queen of the Night. Mozart attains a remarkable balance between

the need for the words to be clear (they are not repeated) and the need to be musically appealing, while still reflecting his characters' contrasting emotions. Pamina's lyricism, expressing love for her mother, is firmly dismissed by Sarastro; for the Queen, he tells her, is 'ein stolzes Weib' ('a proud woman').

Mozart brings back the descending scale of Monostatos's previous entrance as he returns, now dragging in Tamino – who is immediately drawn to Pamina, and she to him. Mozart again coordinates music with the action as Sarastro intervenes and Monostatos is rebuked. This section concludes with another passage from Sarastro, those deep notes again in evidence: he commands the priests to prepare Tamino and Papageno for the trials of initiation into the Brotherhood. Pamina, for the moment, is silenced, and seemingly overlooked. A paean in praise of virtue and justice, sung by the chorus, concludes the act.

Act Two

We have experienced a remarkably wide range of musical styles in Act One; yet Act Two opens with another style altogether. The March of the Priests, composed last along with the Overture, has a ritualistic character reminiscent of sacrificial marches by Gluck, and the March in Act Three of *Idomeneo*.[12] The Act One finale celebrated the grandeur of Sarastro and the discipline imposed on the order he governs, hence the military temper of the music. By contrast, the March of Priests here is hieratic, its orchestration reflecting Mozart's Masonic music and anticipating the Requiem on which he was probably already engaged. The wind instruments include basset horns, bassoons and trombones, as in the Requiem, but also horns and a flute [9].[13]

Thanks to the hieratic style, we know we must take the trials seriously, and they are not much undermined by Papageno's comical objections and all-too-human desire for food and wine. After the March,

---

12 The models in Gluck are in *Alceste* and both of his *Iphigénie* operas.

13 Basset horns are low-pitched clarinets, played by the clarinettists. The parallel chords are typical of Gluck's ritual marches, which also feature the flute.

Sarastro consults a gathering of the Priests; he vouches for Tamino, and the threefold 'Dreimalige Akkorde' resound grandly from the wind ensemble. The Speaker questions whether a prince can withstand such trials; Sarastro's response ('Noch mehr – Er ist Mensch!' ['More than that – he is a man!']) is again followed by the 'Dreimalige Akkorde'. Sarastro then sings a two-part hymn to the Egyptian deities Isis and Osiris [10]. The two stanzas are complementary, but not identical. The chorus repeats the refrain to each stanza, with ethereal harmony, the melody in an inner part.[14] From the March's instrumentation Mozart drops flute, horns and violins; the highest strings are divided violas.

The trial scenes mix rough comedy (mostly in dialogue) with pathos (which demands musical expression). The Two Priests who instruct Tamino and Papageno have to deal with the latter's banter, and so participate in the comedy, as does Tamino (in dialogue). The Priests' duet admonishing the pair to beware the wiles of women would fit happily into an *opera buffa* [11].[15] Mozart's music implies that the misogyny the Priests express should not be taken too literally. Even when trombones join in at the threat of death, the Priests sing *sotto voce,* and the staccato march rhythm of their last words, repeated by the orchestra, remains light in texture, neither hieratic nor particularly threatening.

A worse threat is the arrival of the Three Ladies, who appear for a second quintet with Tamino and Papageno [12]. Yet here too the mood is essentially comic. The men talk only to each other, and Tamino repeatedly tells Papageno to shut up. The Ladies cease their threats and try seduction, to no avail, although Papageno is tempted. The five again unite to sing the moral together, ending: 'Von festem Geiste ist ein Mann, / er denket, was er sprechen kann' ('A man is strong in spirit / who thinks before he speaks'). An off-stage chorus banishes the Ladies; Papageno echoes their departing cries of 'O Weh!' ('Alas!') in a comic faint. The quintet, in G major, ends unusually, on a solo, and in G *minor* – the opera's key of pathos. The 'Dreimalige Akkorde' again resound as the priests lead Tamino and Papageno away.

---

14 The part-writing is altered because the refrains are respectively in the dominant (C) and tonic (F).

15 The duet is marked Allegretto, but two in a bar, so a sprightly tempo.

Monostatos comes upon Pamina asleep. His aria, in two stanzas (the music exactly repeated) evokes the *alla turca* style associated with Osmin in *Die Entführung aus dem Serail*, despite the absence of 'Turkish' percussion [13]. It is night; he asks the moon not to spy on him as he prepares to rape Pamina. This dark deed is prepared in brightly textured music, including piccolo with higher-pitched clarinets and bassoons, and no brass. Monostatos is interrupted by the Queen, who accuses her daughter of betrayal and hands her a dagger to kill Sarastro, silencing her objections by her tremendous second aria [14].[16] This is a single movement in D minor, a key Mozart favoured in contexts of dark, turbulent feelings.[17] This soon leads to her most celebrated passage (the nominal text 'mehr' here is likely to be replaced by 'ah' in performance to ease the singer's task).

Swirling strings evoke the tempest in her heart. Returning grandly to D minor, she launches another sequence (the underlying syllable in the text this time is 'Ban') in a stream of triplets, then a sequential passage using the motif quoted, but not the highest note, before concluding with a ferocious cadence in recitative.

Monostatos has overheard and tries to blackmail Pamina. But even without CCTV, Sarastro or his agents apparently see everything; and he himself enters to banish Monostatos for good. Pamina's plea for her mother is silenced; yet Sarastro dismisses all thought of vengeance in a noble aria [15] that, curiously, shares the

16 It is in the course of the dialogue preceding this aria that the Queen reveals important information about the backstory to the opera and her relationship with her husband. Rarely included in performances, it explains much about the source of the Queen's bitterness and anger. Readers are referred to lines 7–17 on pp. 178 and 179 of the libretto in this guide [Ed.].

17 For example, the Piano Concerto K466 and the Requiem.

form (two musically identical stanzas) elsewhere used for Papageno and Monostatos.

We return to broad comedy, with Papageno's promised wife Papagena appearing in the guise of an old woman. If the structure here appears loose, it is the natural consequence of a plot that engages us – unlike *opera seria* and many contemporary comedies – with a wide range of human and superhuman beings. Light relief is needed after the frenzy of the Queen of the Night and the solemnity of her antagonist Sarastro; it comes in a movement of musical enchantment, the A major trio of the Three Boys, 'Seid uns zum zweiten Mal willkommen' ('We welcome you a second time') [16].[18] The short instrumental refrain has flute and bassoon respectively an octave above and below the violins, which also have a flickering motif suggestive of Tamino's beating heart, as appears earlier in his opening Act One aria. But Tamino must remain silent even when Pamina appears – a far more difficult trial for him than confronting the Three Ladies (although easier for Papageno, as he complacently reminds us after Pamina's departure).

Pamina's aria 'Ach, ich fühl's, es ist verschwunden' ('Alas, I feel that it has vanished') responds to Tamino's apparent rejection. It is in G minor, often the key of despair in Mozart [17]. More important than the key in this unsurpassed expression of pathos are the stark simplicity of the accompaniment and the predominantly falling vocal line, varied by Pamina's repeated reaching for her highest note (bar 6 in music example 17), well below her mother's highest. The wide falling interval (also bar 6) is later heard from flute and oboe, after a flowing passage that seems to stumble when four notes recur at half-speed.[19] As the aria (which some consider Mozart's greatest) draws to a close, slower passagework leads to further wide intervals (astonishing for a singer aged only seventeen, as Anna Gottlieb was said to have been at the premiere in 1791), concluding in singing 'then I shall find peace in death':

---

18 The voices enter in the fifth bar; the first bar is included to show the violin motif.

19 The four notes F–G–A–B flat; see bars 14–15.

Ruh im_ To - de_ sein!   so wird Ruh___   im   To - de sein!

We need reminding of the reason for Tamino's cruel silence. Following a short scene for Papageno, the next one opens with the chorus
and another priestly invocation of the Egyptian deities [18]. They express confidence; so far, the trials have gone well. Tamino is brought
back on stage, and then Pamina, for Sarastro to tell them they must
bid each other a last farewell, an additional twist which we cannot yet
see is well meant. The trio is marked Andante (i.e. medium tempo),
with the time-signature implying two beats in a bar rather than four;
the same as the opening of Act One and the duet for the Second Priest
and Speaker, No. 11 [19]. Pamina, it appears, continues to believe
that this is their final parting; she fails to register the contradiction
between Sarastro telling the couple to prepare for this and the first
words he sings in the trio, 'Ihr werdet froh euch wieder sehn' ('You
will see each other again in joy'). Sarastro joins Tamino in a devout
sentiment, that the gods will protect him (he does not ask anyone to
protect Pamina, although, as will appear later, she is not forgotten).
At the end, Sarastro sings 'Die Stunde schlägt! Wir sehn uns wieder'
('The time has come, we shall meet again!') in his low register, while
the lovers plead for better times to return, and repeat their farewells.
We are left in a state of uncertainty, no bad thing at this juncture in a
dramatic work. Nevertheless, the trio marks what has been perceived
as a problem in the sequence of numbers in the opera, leading to pro-
posals to change their order.[20] It is possible that the trio was a late
addition to the opera, but the evidence is inconclusive and it is best to
retain the ordering as in Mozart's autograph score.

Papageno tries to summon Papagena with his magic bells, launch-
ing another popular song, this time in three stanzas [20], each with a

20 See Peter Branscombe, *W.A. Mozart: Die Zauberflöte* (Cambridge Univer-
    sity Press, 1991), pp. 209–12. It may be significant that the autograph of this
    trio uses the same paper type as the Overture, which was written only just
    before the premiere, and so may have been a late addition. Another proposal
    to change the order of numbers in a Mozart opera is discussed in Gary Kahn
    (ed.), *Le nozze di Figaro* (London: Alma Books, 2011), pp. 85–87.

second part in a dance-like 6/8 metre. The tune repeats, but the glock-enspiel has increasingly elaborate figuration in each successive stanza, and a final flourish in the instrumental coda. The accompaniment is light, the violins doubling the melody two octaves above the voice. Woodwind and horns are added to the third stanza and the coda. At one performance during the initial run in 1791, Mozart amused himself by going backstage and playing Papageno's magic bells from the wings in the wrong place, making it clear to the audience that Schikaneder wasn't playing them himself, to which Schikaneder, experienced trouper as he was, played up with a joke of his own.[21]

Second Finale. The two finales are alike in design, with changes of scene and personnel and a great deal of action, concluding with a chorus. But there is a difference in the manner of their endings, because during the second finale dramatic tensions are resolved: the wicked schemes of the Queen are defeated, loving couples are united and the Three Boys hail a new dawn. It is noteworthy that, despite misogynistic opinions expressed by some of the characters, the chorus in both finales includes women and the implication is clear that Sarastro's order will pass to the benevolent governance of a married couple, Pamina and Tamino.

The second finale is governed by the tonality of the Overture, E flat major, but ranges widely. It starts, like the first finale, with the Three Boys, who are still to intervene further and decisively, twice, in the fate of the characters [21a]. First, they invoke the beauty of dawn. Then, spying Pamina in distress, they realize that she is 'von Sinnen', not in her right mind, distracted by grief. The Three Boys adopt a minor key in which Pamina's lament begins.

The Three Boys comment, then approach her; but at first she does not heed them.[22] They try a new musical pattern (faster and in a triple

---

21 See Mozart's letter to his wife, 8th–9th October 1791, Eisen, op. cit., p. 565.
22 The Three Boys move to C minor, but Pamina raises the emotional temperature along with the key, which rises to G minor, the key of 'Ach, ich fühl's'.

metre), and this time they gain her attention, telling her while they cannot explain Tamino's coldness, they can now lead her to him. The home key (E flat) is restored, and her voice soars joyfully above the Three Boys, sustaining her highest note over four bars, to reach a decisive cadence.

The scene changes to a rugged landscape: two mountains flank the stage for the final trials of fire and water. The music recaptures a hieratic quality; the dotted rhythm and the solemn trombones remind us of the opening of the first finale [21b; compare 8a]. Violins introduce imitative or 'learned' counterpoint, over which a solemn chorale melody is sung in octaves by tenor and bass, the First and Second Man in Armour [21c].[23]

Tamino is preparing for the ordeals of fire and water when Pamina's voice is heard from offstage. The previously austere First and Second Man in Armour cheerfully agree that it is indeed her voice, and wish the pair luck, for they will undertake the ordeals together. The lovers' greeting is a moment of joy taken without fanfare but with the simplest phrases expressing confidence that all will now be well, 'My Tamino/Pamina / Oh, what joy':

But before the trials begin, Pamina has important things to say to Tamino. She will remain at his side and she tells him to play the magic flute, which she recognizes as her father's work, carved in a magical time from an ancient oak. This is another of those free, declamatory yet expressive vocal passages that characterize some of the most moving passages in this opera and point most strongly to the operas of the nineteenth century: Weber, even Wagner. The section concludes with a quartet in which Pamina soars above the three male voices.

---

23 The melody is a penitential Protestant chorale invoking God's help: 'Ach Gott, vom Himmel sieh' darein'. Unlike the Overture, this is not strictly a fugue, but the music nevertheless reflects Mozart's study of J.S. Bach.

An orchestral transition leads to the trial music, set to a uniquely austere march [21d]. Mozart treats the dangers of fire and water without melodrama but with novel instrumental colour; the flute plays the melody, accompanied only by brass, the phrases punctuated by timpani. After passing through fire, the pair sing with a woodwind and string ensemble; the process is repeated for the trial by water. Fanfares and chorus, very much in the style as well as the key (C) of the first finale, greet their victory; and we never hear again the voices of Pamina and Tamino.

Meanwhile, what of Papageno? In despair, he has again forgotten about his magic bells, and tries in vain to summon Papagena with his panpipes. His long solo departs far from the popular idiom of his songs [21e]. Instead it develops an elaborate rondo form, with episodes and a nagging refrain motif to which he and the orchestra continually return:

The key is G major, but the first episode is in E minor, with scurrying violin scales; the second episode uses G minor, Mozart's key of despair again. He tries more frantic piping, to no avail, and is about to hang himself when the Three Boys intervene: 'So lasse deine Glöckchen klingen' ('Then play your little bells'). After a delightful section in which he blames his own foolishness, Papageno sets them ringing once more. The Three Boys slip away and return with the youthful Papagena, whereat these lovers greet one another with a stammer ('Pa – Pa – Pa – Pa – Pa – Pa – Papagena/Papageno' etc.) and anticipate a happy future with a large family. Despite this little comedy, however, Papageno is not a trivial character; his intention to kill himself is no less serious than Pamina's, and Mozart and Schikaneder have here provided a kind of apotheosis of ordinary people, who want only to live their life productively and in peace.

Both couples are united, but we have not heard the last of the Queen of the Night. She and the Three Ladies (now joined by Monostatos) attempt to storm the temple from beneath: they are characterized by a dry march in C minor [21f] and a prayer to the Queen. They are banished by an orchestral uproar, and serenity is

restored in a particularly beautiful transition which finally establishes the opera's principal key, E flat. Sarastro's short oration, 'Die Strahlen der Sonne vertreiben die Nacht' ('The rays of the sun drive the night away'), declaimed with his characteristic wide intervals and deep notes, is followed by a chorus in two movements. Here Mozart strikes a subtly different note from the first finale, where the fanfares were martial, without hieratic trombones. Act Two invokes the same grandeur, starting with a major-key version of music example 21b [21g1]. This yields to a faster tempo, in spirit closer to an *opera buffa* finale. Trumpets reinforce the other instruments and chorus, though no longer playing military fanfares, and trombones continue to support and punctuate the musical texture, but the focus is very much on the chorus, who contrast the sprightly violin opening [21g2] with a lyrical phrase [21g3] as they offer the crown to beauty and wisdom – Pamina and Tamino in priestly garb, the Three Boys not singing, but offering flowers.

A Selective Performance History

Hugo Shirley

Two of Mozart's operas stand out for the richness and complexity of their performance history: *Don Giovanni* and *Die Zauberflöte*. Both works have retained their places in the repertory since their premieres. The course of their reception has been subject to the shifting tides of broader attitudes to Mozart, reflecting to a large degree the dialectic of Mozart the proto-Romantic genius set against Mozart the child of nature. Subsequent generations, meanwhile, have struggled to reconcile comedic and serious elements in both works: elements that, in Mozart's day, coexisted more naturally than they would in later, more straightforwardly polarized times. Both works, additionally, have inspired an array of parodies and spin-offs as well as exerting an influence far beyond the walls of the opera house, proving uniquely fascinating to writers, philosophers, visual artists and film-makers.[1]

With *Die Zauberflöte*, the reception is arguably all the more complicated: it involves coming to grips not only with the exact nature of the opera's subject, but also with its relationship to Mozart's own life as a Freemason. In the late nineteenth century, George Bernard Shaw described *Die Zauberflöte* as 'the ancestor, not only of the Ninth Symphony, but of the Wagnerian allegorical music-drama, with

---

1 In the case of *Die Zauberflöte*, various sequels attempted either to take advantage of the work's popularity or, in the case of Goethe's aborted attempt, to resolve and explore the issues raised by the work. These are summarized in Peter Branscombe (ed.), *W. A. Mozart: 'Die Zauberflöte'* (Cambridge: Cambridge University Press, 1991), pp. 164*ff*.

personified abstractions instead of individual characters as *dramatis personae*'.[2] And that description chimes with the first sentence of Julian Rushton's entry on the work in *The New Grove Dictionary of Opera*: '*Die Zauberflöte*', he writes, 'is an allegory set in no real locality or historical period.'[3] Academic debate has raged meanwhile as to the extent to which the opera is specifically a work about Freemasonry. What are complicated issues in theory become doubly knotty in practice: any production has to deal with this legacy or be accused of ignoring or underplaying it, but productions that set out to fix the work in a geographical locality – invariably Egypt – risk suffocating it in so much mummifying literalism.

Another element that opera directors ignore at their peril is *Die Zauberflöte*'s origins in popular theatre – an especially challenging task in the large theatres that became the norm during the nineteenth century. Any staging, moreover, should try and make a coherent theatrical evening out of a plot apparently awash with mystery and inconsistency – all compounded by the eternal fascination of all of Mozart's late works, written in what we retrospectively like to imagine was the shadow of an impending early death. The work, in the later twentieth century in particular, presents further issues when it comes to gender and race. The libretto's casual sexism is often retained, but the fact that it equates Monastatos's evil with his blackness presents two options: the issue can either be whitewashed by adjusting the text and/or surtitles, or – more controversially, perhaps – retained in the name of faithfulness to the text and historic authenticity. This happened as recently as 2016 with Peter Stein's La Scala production, which featured a blacked-up Monastatos and entourage. Whatever position a production might take, it remains, in the words of Mary Hunter, 'impossible to do the opera without the fundamental opposition between good and evil, the latter represented by a hysterical woman, allied with a black slave'.[4]

2   George Bernard Shaw, *Music in London 1890–1894*, 3 vols. (London: Constable, repr. 1956), vol. 1, p. 295.

3   *The New Grove Dictionary of Opera*, ed. Stanley Sadie, 4 vols. (London: Macmillan, 1992), vol. 1, p. 1215.

4   Mary Hunter, *Mozart's Operas: A Companion* (New Haven and London: Yale University Press, 2008), p. 109.

* * *

Such issues were of course unproblematic in late-eighteenth-century Vienna, where our story begins, only shortly before Mozart's death, at the suburban Freihaus-Theater auf der Wieden.[5] This building, seating some 800 spectators (expanded to 1,000 with addition of an extra tier in 1794) and of unsophisticated rectangular design, was built swiftly in 1787, and had been taken over by Emanuel Schikaneder in mid-1789. Peter Branscombe paints a full picture of the varied theatrical repertory into which *Die Zauberflöte*, billed as 'Eine große Oper' (a grand opera), was introduced on 30th September 1791 – there were operas and *Singspiele*, comic plays as well as works by the grander names of German-speaking theatre.[6]

The cast was a mix of youth and experience: an impressive collection of musico-theatrical all-rounders. They were led by Schikaneder himself, just turned forty, as Papageno – not in his youthful prime, perhaps, but still clearly a good singer as well as 'one of the outstanding men of German theatre at the time'.[7] Sarastro was the twenty-four-year-old Franz Xaver Gerl (1764–1827), a member of Schikaneder's troupe since 1787; Papagena ('ein altes Weib' on the original playbill) was sung by his wife, the former child star Barbara Reisinger (1770–1806). Benedickt Schack (1758–1826), who would also sing the first Don Ottavio in German, created the role of Tamino. Schack had been admired by Leopold Mozart and was a close friend of his son, while his other varied skills included being a

---

5   Not to be confused with Schikaneder's later and still extant Theater an der Wien, which he founded after leaving the Theater auf der Wieden. His new theatre would be the site of the premiere of Beethoven's *Fidelio* and is adorned with a 'Papageno Gate' portraying Schikaneder in his most famous role.

6   Details of the premiere of *Die Zauberflöte* have been exhaustively laid out by Peter Branscombe in his Cambridge Opera Handbook on the opera, op cit. His chapter on its 'Performance and Reception' necessarily helps provide the starting point for this survey. See also H.C. Robbins Landon, *1791: Mozart's Last Year* (London: repr. Flamingo, 1990), pp. 137–47; Otto Erich Deutsch, 'The Première of *Die Zauberflöte*', trans. Anne Ross, *Opera*, July 1956, pp. 404–11.

7   Branscombe, op. cit., p. 145.

fine flautist, bringing the added advantage of his having been theo-retically able to perform Tamino's flute solos himself – although there is no concrete evidence of him actually having done so.

Schack's wife Elisabeth (née Weinhold) sang the Third Lady. The Queen of the Night was sung by Josepha Hofer, née Weber (1759–1819). She was Mozart's sister-in-law and the role was composed for her. Hofer's relationship with the Freihaus-Theater went back to early 1789; she stayed on in Schikaneder's company until 1805, and her later roles included a reprise of the Queen of the Night in Peter von Winter's sequel, *Das Labyrinth, oder Der Kampf mit den Elementen* (*The Labyrinth, or the Struggle of the Elements*), in 1798. The youngest of the principals was the Pamina, Anna Gott-lieb (1774–1856), though now, at seventeen, she was something of a veteran compared to when she created Barbarina in *Le nozze di Figaro* after just turning twelve.

Monastatos was sung by Johann Joseph Nouseul, the oldest mem-ber of the cast, aged forty-nine and an experienced man of the thea-tre, both on the stage (primarily as an actor) and behind the scenes as an administrator. The smaller roles are not quite so well document-ed, but alongside Elisabeth Schack, the First and Second Ladies were Mlles Klöpfer and Hofmann. There is a lack of clarity as regards the various Priests and Speaker. Schikaneder's older brother Urban, a bass, is listed as First Priest (although he is likely to have sung the Second Priest, i.e. the bass rather than the tenor, as we more usually understand it). Herr Winter, stage manager of the theatre, is listed as Speaker, although Branscombe notes that there is no evidence of his having been a singer.[8] The original playbill did not include all the names for the Three Boys, although the first is thought to have been sung by Anna Schikaneder (1746–1818), Urban's daughter and Ema-nuel's niece. It is likely that the trio consisted, as would become an early standard practice, of a mixture of women and boys.

Mozart himself conducted the first two performances. Johann Bap-tist Henneberg (1768–1822), *Kapellmeister* and resident composer of Schikaneder's company from 1790 to 1803, took over after Mozart's performances, having already led many of the rehearsals while the

8   Branscombe, op. cit., p. 148.

composer was otherwise engaged with the premiere of *La clemenza di Tito* in Prague. *Die Zauberflöte* proved an enormous success for Schikaneder and his theatre, with performances packed into the schedule for the following months and revivals over the next ten years. Mozart himself reports nipping backstage unexpectedly to play the glockenspiel in a letter of 7th October, an episode that would enter the popular imagination through a scene in Peter Shaffer's *Amadeus*.[9]

Unfortunately little has survived to help us provide an accurate picture of how the first *Zauberflöte* looked, although an engraving by Josef and Peter Schaffer from 1795 for the trials by fire and water show a familiar juxtaposition of threatening nature and architectural order. We know that Schikaneder spared no expense in realizing the special effects that would be part of the work's appeal. Mozart would remark ruefully about his mother-in-law – in comments that would echo throughout the centuries regarding those unable to appreciate the serious side of the work – that she would 'see the opera but not hear it'.[10]

* * *

Prague was the first city outside Vienna to see the work, over a year after its premiere, with a performance on 25th October 1792 at the Nostitz Theatre (where *Don Giovanni* had its premiere four years earlier). It later appeared too at the Thun Theatre in the Malá Strana, with enlarged chorus and a contingent of children brought in to play animals. The following year saw performances proliferate across German-speaking lands, with the opera appearing on a dozen stages (including Leipzig, Munich, Dresden and Frankfurt am Main) in 1793. Another two dozen cities followed in 1794, including Hanover, Berlin, Amsterdam, Nuremberg and Cologne. Although these performances, as well as those in Ofen (Buda), Pest and Warsaw in 1793, were in German, variations to this started to appear.

9   Robbins Landon, op. cit., p. 144. See also Julian Rushton's article in this guide, p. 38.
10 Emily Anderson (ed. and trans.), *The Letters of Mozart and His Family*, 3rd edn. (London: Macmillan Press, 1985), p. 968.

In 1794, Prague saw performances in Italian (as part of the carnival season) and even Czech. The work turned up in French in Brunswick after first being heard there in German. Performances further afield included those in the (now) Romanian cities of Timişoara (Temeschburg as it then was) and Sibiu (Hermannstadt), as well as Eisenstadt in Austria. The opera made it to Russia (St Petersburg) in 1797, then Moscow in 1801. As it crossed linguistic boundaries it tended to be translated: that Moscow performance was in Russian, while other performances in Warsaw (1802) and Poznań (1805) were in Polish. Its first appearance in Stockholm (1812) and Copenhagen (1816) followed suit by being in the vernacular, as did its eventual first performance in Italy, in Milan, in 1816.[11]

Changes of language also meant changes to bring *Die Zauberflöte* into line with local operatic expectations. The 1794 Italian staging in Prague, given by the same company, Guardisoni's, that had commissioned and premiered *Don Giovanni*, saw the addition of recitative, as well as various reassignments of numbers. But even in German, adjustments inevitably crept in, as was the case in Weimar where Christian August Vulpius created an influential three-act version described by Branscombe as 'at once clumsy […] and fussy'. Although a clear bowdlerization of the original, Vulpius's version is notable for introducing ideas of the sort that would regularly crop up in productions a couple of centuries later: Sarastro is made into the Queen of the Night's brother-in-law, for example, and retires from his position to give way to Tamino.[12] Significantly, this version, performed some eighty-two times between 1794 and 1817, coincided with Goethe's management of the Weimar theatre, and Vulpius's liberties with the text and imaginative additional details could have inspired Goethe's own unfinished sequel, *Der Zauberflöte zweyter Theil*.

Several other early productions seem to have taken liberties with the libretto, but, as with *Don Giovanni*, it was *Die Zauberflöte*'s

---

11 For specific details of first performances, see Alfred Loewenberg, *The Annals of Opera 1597–1940*, 3rd edn. (London: John Calder, 1978), pp. 494–98; Branscombe, op. cit., pp. 160–62.

12 Branscombe, op. cit., p. 163.

arrival in Paris that marked the start of the biggest changes. With *Die Zauberflöte* these were inflicted right from the very start in the French capital, while the version that appeared at the Paris Opéra for the first time on 20th August 1801 simultaneously marks the start of a reception strand that focused explicitly on the mysterious, Egyptian elements of the work. Renamed *Les Mystères d'Isis* (and quickly in turn dubbed *Les Misères d'ici*), it retitled several characters with more exotic names, reworked the libretto into four acts and rearranged the score to include music not only from *Le nozze di Figaro*, *Don Giovanni* and *La clemenza di Tito*, but also from Haydn's 'Drumroll' Symphony.[13]

* * *

Berlin, two decades after it first saw the opera, staged what is arguably the most influential production of all, at least in terms of cementing the *Zauberflöte* iconography. This 1816 staging featured designs by Karl Friedrich Schinkel, the man appointed to impose architectural law and order over the Prussian capital. This brought Mozart's opera into a world of rationality – right down to the evenly arrayed stars that adorn the famous backdrop for the Queen of the Night's scenes – and Egyptian designs pitted against hints of sublime Nature. The following year Goethe commissioned new designs for Weimar by Friedrich Beuther,[14] while the 1818 Munich production designed by Simon Quaglio (1795–1878) followed the trend (and replaced Joseph Quaglio's 1793 designs).

As John Allison has noted, Schinkel's designs, though replaced relatively swiftly by those of his disciple Karl Friedrich Thiele, proved influential up to the present day.[15] They are regularly referenced in other productions and were even pointedly recreated in August Everding's Berlin Staatsoper production (premiered under

---

13 A recording of this version, conducted by Diego Fasolis, was issued on the Glossa label in 2015.

14 Gernot Gruber, *Mozart and Posterity*, trans. R.S. Furness (London: Quartet Books, 1991), p. 69.

15 John Allison, 'Paintings that Sing', *Opera*, November 2014, pp. 1378–79.

the baton of Daniel Barenboim on 14th December 1994 and still in the company's repertory at the time of writing). A version of Schinkel's design was also seen in London as late as 1938, when Thomas Beecham brought the opera to Covent Garden in scenery 'lent by the Charlottenburg Opera in Berlin'.[16] The scenery wasn't the only thing borrowed from German-speaking lands on that occasion: Richard Tauber led an impressive international cast as Tamino, joined by Gerhard Hüsch as Papageno, Tiana Lemnitz as Pamina and Erna Berger as the Queen of the Night, all three of whom also featured on Beecham's important 1937–38 recording of the opera made in the German capital with the Berlin Philharmonic Orchestra.

But we're getting ahead of ourselves. London's first engagement with the work had been some 130 years previously. Its first fully documented appearance in the English capital was at the King's Theatre, Haymarket in 1811 where it was forced by licensing conditions to be performed as *Il flauto magico*, a version in which Mozart and Schikaneder's characters were shoehorned into an Italian opera mould. 'The dialogue was rendered in Italian couplets,' notes theatre historian Sarah Lenton, 'and, in his new tongue, Tamino became an Italian noble prince, Pamina a noble Italian princess and Sarastro a run-of-the-mill High Priest.'[17] The musicologist Rachel Cowgill has shown, however, what currency the opera had more generally even before this date, not just in her discovery of a hand-written translation of the libretto – replete with fascinating allegorical introduction – possibly planned for the production at the King's Theatre, but also in her research into where and when arias were interpolated into other shows up until 1814.[18] It has also been suggested that *The Daughter of the Air*, billed as a 'Persian drama'

16 Rosenthal, op. cit., p. 532.

17 Sarah Lenton, 'Staging the *Flute*' in Royal Opera House programme for 2002–3 Season, p. 36.

18 Rachel Cowgill, 'New Light and the Man of Might: Revisiting Early Interpretations of *Die Zauberflöte*', in Rachel Cowgill, David Cooper and Clive Brown (eds.), *Art and Ideology in European Opera: Essays in Honour of Julian Rushton* (Woodbridge: The Boydell Press, 2010), pp. 194–221. On this subject, see also Branscombe, op. cit., pp. 155–56.

with music by Mozart and seen at John Dibdin's Sadler's Wells Theatre in 1800, was in fact a version of *Die Zauberflöte*.[19]

The opera continued to be produced in Italian in London, however, for much of the nineteenth century, including a version that was heard in a Royal Command performance for Queen Victoria on 10th July 1851. It featured a star cast, including, in Pauline Viardot as Papagena, the sort of luxury casting that would arguably have to wait until Otto Klemperer's famous 1964 recording to be matched.[20] As Branscombe notes, quoting a long review in *The Times* of the event, it seems only to have cemented the general view that had solidified with regard to Mozart and many of his operas as the nineteenth century ran its course – that the composer's divine genius had had to stoop to set the words of inferior artists. As with *Don Giovanni*, a mid-nineteenth century tendency towards both operatic piety and staid grandeur seems to have found it difficult to come to terms with works composed for more modest theatres and eighteenth-century sensibilities.

Though this royal performance had been in Italian – and performances of *Il flauto magico* remained the norm – there were exceptions. On 27th May 1833, *Die Zauberflöte* kicked off a German season at the Royal Opera House and included among its cast a twenty-eight-year-old Wilhelmine Schröder-Devrient as Pamina (alternating with performances as Beethoven's Leonore) who was dramatically compelling if, apparently, somewhat wayward vocally. Wagner's favourite singer had made her operatic debut in 1820, aged only seventeen, as Pamina in Vienna and must certainly have presented a very different portrayal of the role from those that are the norm today. Another guest company presented the opera as part of a German season at Covent Garden in May 1842, but struggled apparently against London's predisposition towards Italian

19 Dennis Arundell, *The Story of Sadler's Wells 1683–1964* (London: Hamish Hamilton, 1965), p. 61.
20 Klemperer's Three Ladies included Elisabeth Schwarzkopf and Christa Ludwig. Karl Böhm's almost contemporaneous Deutsche Grammophon recording matches such starry casting at the other end of the spectrum, with James King and Martti Talvela as the Two Men in Armour.

opera.[21] And still as late as 1888 at Covent Garden it was subject, in performances conducted by the Italian-born Alberto Randegger, to the interpolation of a ballet using Mozart's chamber music. Even Thomas Beecham's performances at Drury Lane in spring 1914 included composed recitatives.[22]

Die Zauberflöte's progress over the Atlantic was relatively slow, and although it has been suggested there was a performance in Philadelphia as early as 1832, this remains unsubstantiated. The first New York performance dates from 17th April the following year, when it was given at the Park Theatre in an English version. German and Italian versions followed in 1855 and 1859 respectively.[23] Throughout the nineteenth century, though, its popularity in German-speaking lands was remarkable, with Vienna seeing the work more than 600 times throughout the century – with some 450 performances at the Court Opera and 150 at the Theater an der Wien.[24] Later the opera was included in Munich's important drive to remove accrued traditions of the nineteenth century when it was given a new production there on 30th April 1898. It was conducted by Richard Strauss, but was not, of course, able to boast the widely admired continuo playing that had distinguished his conducting of the Da Ponte operas.[25] Nor was it staged, as those productions had been, in the baroque Cuvilliés-Theater: it was unveiled at the much larger Nationaltheater.[26]

Strauss's great contemporary Gustav Mahler presided over a new production in Vienna not long afterwards. Mahler's first performances of *Die Zauberflöte* as part of his Viennese reign (29th May 1897) drew praise from critics but also calls for reform: to do away with additions to the dialogue that had built up over a century of performance (making it resemble, according to one commentator, a 'parody of Offenbach') and restore the text as it appears in the

---

21 Rosenthal, op. cit., p. 56.
22 Rosenthal, op. cit., p. 227; Branscombe, op. cit., p. 171.
23 Loewenberg, op. cit., p. 498.
24 Branscombe op. cit., p. 168.
25 Franz Trenner, *Richard Strauss Chronik* (Vienna; Verlag Dr. Richard Strauss), p. 166.
26 Gruber, op. cit., p. 185.

libretto. This Mahler instigated in time for a revival the following year.[27] The production that Alfred Roller designed for Mahler in 1906 followed previous ones designed by Anton de Pian (1818 at the Kärtnertortheater) and Josef Hoffmann (1869).

Staged to complete the programme for a 150th-anniversary celebration at the Hofoper, Roller's production was not entirely new and had to make do with many of Hoffmann's existing sets. But he was able to instigate such changes as a more dramatic entrance for the Queen of the Night: she now rose up from between parting rocks, rather than, as before, simply entering from the wings. The overall effect seems to have been one of Egyptian monumentalism giving way to abstraction and symbolism, a combination that led to charges that it lacked fairy-tale naivety.[28]

And here we encounter an expression of one of the primary difficulties with *Die Zauberflöte* in terms of staging the work in large theatres. In her guide to Mozart's operas, Mary Hunter reproduces a photograph from a production at the Metropolitan Opera in New York, which, she notes, 'make it look like the grandest of grand operas, complete with mechanical elephant and biblical era costumes and sets'.[29] The tendency for literalism and spectacle reaches what might be seen as a sort of apogee in a production that was apparently staged in Egypt at the pyramids in 1912.[30]

But around this time we also see important developments in the work's broader reception. Mahler, we are told by Gernot Gruber, viewed it as akin to a German mystery play,[31] and in German-speaking lands a new fascination seems to have arisen across a broad range of artists throughout the 1910s. It was at the end of the decade that Max Slevogt offered his own interpretation – a kind of free-form artistic 'staging' of it – in the extensive sketches he made

27 Henry-Louis de La Grange, *Gustav Mahler: Vienna: The Years of Challenge (1897–1904)* (Oxford, Oxford University Press, 1995), pp. 32–33, p. 72.

28 Henry-Louis de La Grange, *Gustav Mahler: Vienna: Triumph and Disillusion (1904–1907)* (Oxford: Oxford University Press, 1999), pp. 338–40.

29 Hunter, op. cit., p. 103.

30 Loewenberg, op. cit., p. 498.

31 Gruber, op. cit., p. 186.

in a facsimile copy of the libretto.[32] The same decade saw Richard Strauss and Hugo von Hofmannsthal produce the opera *Die Frau ohne Schatten*, which they saw as bearing a certain analogy to *Die Zauberflöte*, as *Rosenkavalier* had to *Le nozze di Figaro*. Hofmannsthal also produced his short story on the same ideas, and both opera and novella would be caught up in the writer's attempts to re-establish an ideal Austrian identity following the collapse of the Austro-Hungarian Empire. The artistic and intellectual heart was to be situated in the newly founded Salzburg Festival, with Mozart – and in particular his *Zauberflöte*, repositioned as a fruit of the Austrian baroque – at its centre.[33] It has also been argued that Arthur Schnitzler's 1926 *Eine Traumnovelle* is loosely based on Mozart's opera, inviting us to draw a link going as far forward as Stanley Kubrick's final film, *Eyes Wide Shut* (1999).[34]

* * *

The early decades of the twentieth century saw a breakthrough for the work's UK reception. A 1911 production staged in Cambridge used a new translation by the Cambridge professor Edward Dent, modest resources and a mixture of amateur and professional performers. It proved, as the critic of *The Musical Times* wrote: 'first, that [*The Magic Flute*] is an effective opera, granted intelligent management; secondly, that an elaborate work like this can be admirably given by amateurs; and thirdly, that good English is

32 For a fascinating interpretation of Slevogt's sketches see Carolyn Abbate, *In Search of Opera* (Princeton: Princeton University Press, 2001), pp. 58-62. Earlier in the same chapter, 'Magic Flute, Nocturnal Sun', Abbate also discusses Rudolf Heinz's *Silberglöckchen, Zauberflöten* (1992), 'collaborative book by a philosopher and a radical feminist theatre artist who is also an opera singer', as well as other literary responses to the opera that see darkness and depth beneath the surface of its Enlightenment optimism.

33 See Hugo Shirley, 'The "Frau" and the Festival', *Opera*, July 2011, pp. 772–79.

34 In Chapter 5 of his *Undertones of Insurrection* (Lincoln and London: Nebraska University Press, 1993), Marc Weiner explores the different ways in which Schnitzler's *Traumnovelle* and Hofmannsthal's libretto for Strauss's *Die Frau ohne Schatten* use *Die Zauberflöte* a source.

an excellent language for opera'.[35] The opera would, in fact, be performed in English at Covent Garden for the next half-century.

The post-World War Two period was a particularly rich period in and around London for productions. In a review of the new production at Sadler's Wells which opened on 9th August 1967, Harold Rosenthal noted that it was the eighth staging London had seen in two decades (if one admitted Glyndebourne into the capital's orbit) – a period that had seen the opera performed some 245 times.[36] Glyndebourne's own first production, directed by Carl Ebert with designs by Hamish Wilson and conducted by Fritz Busch, opened on 27th May 1935. It was replaced, on 19th July 1956, by a second Ebert staging (this time with designs by Oliver Messel), conducted by Vittorio Gui and with a cast including a young Joan Sutherland as First Lady, Pilar Lorengar as Pamina and Geraint Evans as Papageno. In the capital meanwhile, those Royal Opera House productions included a staging on 19th January 1956 for the Mozart bicentennial year conducted by Rafael Kubelík, directed by Christopher West and designed by John Piper ('a very serious and solemn affair),[37] and one masterminded by Otto Klemperer (who directed, with Christopher West, as well as conducted) and designed by Georg Eisler (4th January 1962), which also featured Sutherland, here promoted to Queen of the Night (although transposing her arias down by a semi-tone and tone respectively).[38]

Peter Hall's production, conducted by Georg Solti at its opening on 5th July 1966, was deemed by Rosenthal to be the most successful of Covent Garden's post-war efforts.[39] As with the previous production, Geraint Evans and Joan Carlyle led the cast as Papageno and Pamina, here joined by others including John Wakefield (Tamino) and Sylvia Geszty (Queen of the Night). The fact that it featured a blacked-up John Dobson as Monastatos drew comment from Rosenthal only inasmuch as the director seems to have given the slaves in his charge

---

35 Quoted in Branscombe, op. cit., p. 170.
36 *Opera*, October 1967, p. 844.
37 Rosenthal, op. cit., p. 656.
38 *Opera*, February 1962, pp. 133*ff*.
39 *Opera*, August 1966, p. 669.

similar make-up, whereas only Monostatos is specified in the libretto as being black. Rosenthal cited Otto Erich Deutsch's 1956 article on the premiere in *Opera*, where the veteran Mozartian noted that the slaves referred to their master as their 'tormentor, the eavesdropping moor', suggesting that they saw him as racially other.[40]

After the previous production had been sung (and spoken) in German by an almost exclusively Anglophone cast – apparently at Klemperer's insistence – the new staging was in a new English translation by Adrian Mitchell, which Rosenthal nevertheless declared inferior to Dent's classic version. Sadler's Wells Opera's new 1967 production (the previous one, dating from 1955, was directed by George Devine, designed by Motley and conducted by Rudolf Schwarz)[41] also incited Rosenthal's wrath for favouring the same new translation over Dent's. Frank Hauser's production, designed by Sam Kirkpatrick and conducted by Bryan Balkwill, didn't fare much better, either, described as 'a generally tedious, unenchanting and visually unrewarding *Magic Flute*'.[42]

Anthony Besch's new 'natural, unfussy staging' in the production for the newly renamed English National Opera at the Coliseum eight years later elicited a much warmer response (16th January 1975). It was praised for its fidelity to the libretto's stage directions and was declared 'able to encompass both the magical and the masonic sides of the ever-perplexing story'. In the next sentence of his *Opera* review Alan Blyth comments revealingly on the balance of comedy and seriousness that needs always to be carefully struck in this work: 'If it is, at times, a little short on down-to-earth humour, that for me is a fault on the right side: too many antics have infected the Papageno scenes in too many productions, all done in the holy name of Schikaneder.'[43] Echoing a complaint Rosenthal had made about the Hall production, Blyth bemoaned the fact that Monastatos's slaves were again in black make-up like their master, suggesting that it removed the necessary sense of contrast.[44]

---

40 Deutsch, op. cit., p. 409.
41 Arundell, op. cit., p. 238.
42 *Opera*, October 1967, pp. 844–45
43 *Opera*, March 1975, p. 303.
44 *Opera*, March 1975, p. 307

The matter of race came to the fore in an altogether happier way with the arrival of Nicholas Hytner's 1988 production at the Coliseum, designed by Bob Crowley. When it opened on 30th March, conducted by Iván Fischer, it featured a black Tamino in Thomas Randle and a white Monostatos. Throughout its twenty-five years as a staple on the Coliseum stage, Hytner's production featured a variety of Taminos, but the whiteness of the Monostatos remained, a reimagining of the character as, in Martin Hoyle's memorable phrase, 'nothing so much as Pooh-bah with libido'.[45]

At Covent Garden, meanwhile, Colin Davis conducted the first performance of a new production by August Everding, designed by Jürgen Rose, on 15th February 1979, with Thomas Allen as Papageno and Ileana Cotrubas as Pamina, plus a couple of impressive Wagnerians in smaller roles in the shape of Alberto Remedios (First Man in Armour) and Donald McIntyre (Speaker). It was replaced by Martin Duncan's production in 1993, a co-production with Scottish Opera, conducted by Andrew Parrott. That in turn was succeeded by David McVicar's 2003 production, with designs by John Macfarlane that emphasized the work's status as an exploration of Enlightenment values. It too was conducted by Colin Davis at its first night (25th January 2003), and featured Simon Keenlyside as Papageno, Dorothea Röschmann as Pamina and Diana Damrau as Queen of the Night; Thomas Allen, now fully initiated into Sarastro's world, sang the Speaker. Monastatos was again not distinguished by race, but rather as an ineffectual fop, who seemed to have misunderstood the edicts of the Enlightenment in a way similar to that in which Beckmesser misunderstands the rules of singing in Wagner's *Die Meistersinger von Nürnberg.*

McVicar's staging, like Hytner's at the Coliseum, immediately established itself as a staple of the company's repertory, racking up over fifty performances in its first decade. Glyndebourne, meanwhile, had produced a classic of its own in John Cox's production in designs by David Hockney, three years after the latter had scored a great success at the Sussex festival with *The Rake's Progress*, and it became most affectionately remembered.

45 *Opera*, May 1988, p. 614.

It opened on 28th May 1978 conducted by Andrew Davis, with a cast including Benjamin Luxon (Papageno) and Isobel Buchanan (Pamina). In *Opera* Charles Osborne described it as 'a *Flute* that captures perfectly that balance between fantasy and reality'.[46] It was televised and in only two seasons (it was revived in 1980) had totted up over forty performances at Glyndebourne and on its tour. The Peter Sellars production designed by Adrianne Lobel that replaced it a decade later – relocating much of the action under a freeway in California, and with all the dialogue cut at its first appearances at the festival – caused a stir in a different way, dividing critics and eliciting boos at its opening night.[47] Subsequent performances at the festival, sung now in English and with the dialogue restored in a translation by Alice Goodman at its sole revival the following year, still failed to meet with approval from most critics or audiences.

Productions outside the United Kingdom in the post-war years have encompassed a variety of styles, and there has been an emerging tendency to explore the work's more serious aspects. Even at the Salzburg Festival, where spectacle had often been given priority in *Zauberflöte* stagings, there was an increasing desire to 'give equal and proper weight to the work's disparate elements',[48] as exemplified in the 1978 production in the Felsenreitschule by Jean-Pierre Ponnelle, which used the newly published Neue Mozart-Ausgabe edition of the score and restored many of the traditional cuts. Nonetheless, that spectacle could still have its place was demonstrated by Grand Magic Circus's Jérôme Savary in a hugely successful production designed by Michel Lebois at the open-air Bregenz Festival in 1985, where 'everything moves, everything revolves… there are spitting fires, sulphurous clouds, trapdoors opening and closing, flying machines hovering high in the air, fabulous creatures swimming in from below across the lake', according to Gotthard Böhm in *Die Bühne* in August of the same year.[49]

---

46 *Opera*, Festival Edition 1978, p. 20.
47 *Opera*, July 1990, p. 976.
48 Rudolph Angermüller, *Mozart's Operas* (New York: Rizzoli, 1988), p. 248.
49 Quoted in ibid., p. 257.

Restoring much of the often previously cut dialogue, however, was by now fast becoming a common feature, as for example in Karl-Ernst and Ursel Herrmann's swift-moving production with minimal sets at the Salzburg Landestheater in 1991 (and later also that year at La Monnaie in Brussels), which featured a particularly young cast and originally an actor who could sing (Ernst Theo Herrmann), rather than a singer who could act, as Papageno. A production by Axel Manthey at Ludwigsburg in 1992, shortly before his early death three years later, presented a naive and especially joyous vision of the work which ended in a riot of primary colours and which has been preserved on DVD. Pierre Audi's much revived production with exotic African tribal-influenced sets by the Dutch painter Karel Appel first appeared at the Nederlandse Opera in Amsterdam in 1995 and is also available on DVD. Of interest is that this recording was made at its 2006 appearance at the Salzburg Festival (conducted by Riccardo Muti), where it was a late replacement for a new Graham Vick production which had been seen at the festival the previous year, but which seemed to have proved too controversial for the Festival to countenance mounting in Mozart's 250th anniversary year (*inter alia*, its portrayal of Sarastro was apparently deemed too negative).

More recently, productions have become increasingly deconstructed. Stagings directed by Damiano Michieletto in designs by Paolo Fantin at La Fenice in 2016 and by Neil Armfield in designs by Dale Ferguson at Lyric Opera of Chicago in 2017 have framed the opera, respectively, in an Italian schoolroom with Sarastro and Pagageno as headmaster and janitor and as an entertainment staged by three boys at the suburban Chicago home of their expatriate Austrian parents. And a new Graham Vick production, designed by Stuart Nunn, at the Macerata Opera Festival in the summer of 2018 featured a bulldozer on stage and was denounced by right-wing critics as an attack on Italy's immigration policy. There seems to be no end to the ways in which the work can be adapted.

* * *

One of the many special features of *Die Zauberflöte* is that it has for so long exerted a fascination for creative artists from beyond the operatic world. David Hockney's highly successful involvement at Glyndebourne in 1978 is far from being an isolated example. For the 1929 production at Berlin's Krolloper, the eminent Bauhaus artist Ewald Dülberg (1888–1933) provided abstract designs for his own production, which was conducted by Otto Klemperer. Oskar Kokoschka, whom Richard Strauss and Hugo von Hofmannsthal had hoped would provide designs for their *Die Frau ohne Schatten*, was invited by Wilhelm Furtwängler to design Max Graf's 1955 production at the Salzburg Festival. (Kokoschka provided designs, too, for another production directed by Graf seen in Geneva and Chicago in 1965 and 1966 respectively.) The USA also saw a famous production designed by Marc Chagall, for the first season of the new Metropolitan Opera in New York (1966/67), where the artist also furnished the theatre's grand foyer with vast *Zauberflöte*-themed murals for its opening. Maurice Sendak provided colourful and distinctive designs for Frank Corsaro's 1980 Houston Grand Opera production, replaced in 1997 by one designed by Gerald Scarfe. As previously mentioned, Karel Appel's designs for Pierre Audi in Amsterdam from 1996 were widely seen when the production was given elsewhere. And in 2005 another significant artist tackled the work: that was the year that William Kentridge's production opened at La Monnaie in Brussels. Exploiting his characteristic 'drawings for projection' technique, it framed the opera within, among other things, a critique of imperialism.[50]

The work has also provided fascination for film directors. Ingmar Bergman's 1975 film – produced in Swedish as *Trollflöjten* – playfully intercut behind-the-scenes action, including shots of Sarastro studying the score of *Parsifal*: an image that reveals a great deal about how this role, in particular, has accumulated gravitas since it was created by the twenty-four-year-old Xaver

---

50 For a more comprehensive survey of artists engaged with productions of *Die Zauberflöte*, see Allison, op. cit., pp. 1378–92.

Gerl.[51] Kenneth Branagh's 2006 film, unveiled at the Venice Film Festival in the city's La Fenice opera house, is altogether more fantastical, given a specific historical dimension by being set against the background of World War One. A hit production in Germany exploited projections and the aesthetic language of early cinema when director Barrie Kosky joined forces with the theatre company 1927 in a wildly imaginative and innovative staging that has travelled widely since it was unveiled on 25th November 2012 at Berlin's Komische Oper, where Walter Felsenstein's 1954 production, with lavish baroque designs by Rudolf Heinrich, had half a century earlier proved such a big success. At the other end of the spectrum, Peter Brook's delicately distilled *Une Flûte enchantée* presented the work, with just piano accompaniment, as a gentle human parable with an African slant, using set and props consisting of little more than a few lengths of bamboo. It was first seen at Brook's Théâtre des Bouffes du Nord in Paris in 2013 before touring.

English National Opera's current production, directed by Simon McBurney and designed by Michael Levine, seems to reflect characteristics from both the Kosky and the Brook productions: barriers between audience and stage broken down, an orchestra raised to stalls level and involved in the action, an essentially empty stage enlivened by improvised props and projections 'drawn' in real time. It was first seen in Amsterdam before coming to the London Coliseum on 7th November 2013 – Gergely Madaras conducted a cast including Devon Guthrie (Pamina), Ben Johnson (Tamino) and Roland Wood as a down-and-out Papageno. Critical reaction to the production, split at first, has grown more universally positive with further revivals, showing how conceptions of a production of *Die*

51 See Albert Ehrnrooth, 'An Operatic Lantern', *Opera*, December 2018, p.1485. A possible significance of the shot in the film showing the singer of Sarastro (Ulrik Cold) reading the score of *Parsifal* has not been widely recognized. Bergman makes it explicit in his film that Sarastro leaves the Brotherhood at the end of the opera and resigns the leadership of the Order to Tamino and Pamina. As in *Parsifal*, a religious or quasi-religious organization receives new leadership and fresh hope for the future, here a man and woman united and strengthened by their love for each other (Ed.).

Zauberflöte can change, especially as a new staging gradually establishes itself against the cherished memory of a predecessor.

Different productions come and go, and critics invariably judge them not only on their own merits but on their potential to turn into staples of a particular opera house's repertory. For *Die Zauberflöte*, according to the website operabase.com, is second in global popularity only to Verdi's *La traviata*. It is work that can be staged in theatres large and small, whose name is immediately recognizable, whose melodies have woven their way into the broader cultural world and whose comedic elements chime with multiple related European comedic traditions – whether the Viennese Hanswurst, Italian *commedia dell'arte* or even England's Punch and Judy. No opera house can afford to have the opera absent from its repertory for long, while we will never run out of directors to face those challenges outlined at the start of this chapter. They might be doomed all to fail in one way or another, but surely true operatic enlightenment lies in rejoicing in the richness of those attempts, and in the fact that the quest for a perfect *Zauberflöte* will for ever remain illusory.

Thematic Guide

Themes from the opera have been identified by the numbers in square brackets in the article on the music, pp. 25–41. These numbers are also printed at corresponding points in the libretto, so that the words can be related to the musical themes.

[3] TAMINO
Larghetto

Dies Bild - nis ist be-zau-bernd schön, wid noch kein Au-ge je ge sehn.

[4a] **Allegro maestoso**

(strings)　　(+ horns)　　(+ bassoons)

crescendo

[4b] QUEEN OF THE NIGHT

O zitt - re nicht, mein lie - ber Sohn

[4c] QUEEN OF THE NIGHT
Andante

Zum Lei - den bin ich aus-er - ko ren, denn mei-ne Toch-ter feh-let mir

[5a] **Allegro**　tr

PAPAGENO

Hm! hm! hm! hm!__ hm! hm! hm!

hm!__ hm! hm! hm! hm!__ hm! hm!__ hm! hm!

[5b] **Andante**

Clarinets (+ violins, pizz.)

THREE LADIES *sotto voce*

p dolce　Bassoon

DreiKnäb-chen, jung, schön, hold, und wei-se

[6] **Allegro molto**

MONOSTATOS

Du fei - nes Täub - chen nur her -

PAMINA

ein. O wel - che Mar - ter, wel - che Pein!

[7] **Andantino**

PAMINA

Bei Män - nern, wel - che Lie - be

füh-len, fehlt auch__ ein gu - tes Her - ze nicht.

63

DIE ZAUBERFLÖTE

65

Die Zauberflöte

Die Zauberflöte

Opera in two acts
by Wolfgang Amadeus Mozart

Libretto by Emanuel Schikaneder
English translation by Kenneth Chalmers of the
complete text from the Neue Mozart-Ausgabe*

Die Zauberflöte was first performed at the Freihaus-Theater auf der Wieden, Vienna, on 30th September 1791. It was first performed in Britain at The King's Theatre, Haymarket, on 6th June 1811. The first performance in the United States was at the Park Theatre, New York, on 17th April 1833.

THE CHARACTERS

Tamino, *a prince*	tenor
Papageno, *a birdcatcher*	baritone
Three Ladies, *attendants to the Queen of the Night*	sopranos, mezzo-soprano
Queen of the Night	soprano
Monostatos, *a Moor in the service of Sarastro*	tenor
Pamina, *daughter of the Queen of the Night*	soprano
Three Boys	sopranos, alto (female or boys)
Speaker	bass
Sarastro, *High Priest of Isis and Osiris*	bass
Two Priests	tenor, bass
Papagena	soprano
Two Men in Armour	tenor, bass

Slaves, chorus of priests, Sarastro's subjects

* This edition is taken from Mozart's autograph score and Schikaneder's printed libretto of 1791. It contains all the original dialogue of the opera, including sections rarely performed on stage or on recordings.

Ouvertüre [0a, 0b]

ERSTER AKT

Erster Auftritt

Das Theater ist eine felsige Gegend, hie und da mit Bäumen überwachsen; auf beiden Seiten sind gangbare Berge, nebst einem runden Tempel.

Tamino kommt in einem prächtigen javonischen Jagdkleide rechts von einem Felsen herunter, mit einem Bogen, aber ohne Pfeil; eine Schlange verfolgt ihn.

Nr. 1 Introduktion [1a]

TAMINO
    Zu Hilfe! Zu Hilfe! Sonst bin ich verloren, [1b]
    der listigen Schlange zum Opfer erkoren.
    Barmherzige Götter! Schon nahet sie sich!
    Ach rettet mich! Ach schützet mich!

(Er fällt in Ohnmacht; sogleich öffnet sich die Pforte des Tempels; drei verschleierte Damen kommen heraus, jede mit einem silbernen Wurfspieß.)

DIE DREI DAMEN
    Stirb, Ungeheu'r, durch unsre Macht! [1c]
    Triumph! Triumph! Sie ist vollbracht,
    die Heldentat. Er ist befreit
    durch unsers Armes Tapferkeit.

ERSTE DAME *(ihn betrachtend)*
    Ein holder Jüngling, sanft und schön.

ZWEITE DAME
    So schön, als ich noch nie gesehn.

Overture [0a, 0b]

ACT ONE

Scene 1

The scene is a rocky landscape overgrown with trees here and there; on both sides are mountains with walkable paths; next to them a round temple.

Tamino, wearing a splendid Javanese hunting costume, enters stage right, coming down from a rock; he has a bow but no arrows; a serpent is chasing him.

No. 1 Introduction   [1a]

TAMINO
    Help! Help! Or else I am lost.   [1b]
    I'll fall victim to this cunning serpent.
    Merciful gods! It's getting closer.
    Rescue me! Save me!

(He faints; the door of the temple immediately opens; three veiled ladies emerge, each carrying a silver javelin.)

THE THREE LADIES
    Die, monster, by our power!   [1c]
    Triumph! Triumph! The heroic deed
    is done. By the valour of our arms
    he has been rescued.

FIRST LADY *(gazing at him)*
    A gracious young man, gentle and handsome.

SECOND LADY
    More handsome than I have ever seen before.

DRITTE DAME
Ja, ja! Gewiss zum Mahlen schön.

ALLE DREI
Würd' ich mein Herz der Liebe weih'n,
so müsst' es dieser Jüngling sein.
Lasst uns zu unsrer Fürstin eilen,
ihr diese Nachricht zu erteilen.
Vielleicht, dass dieser schöne Mann
die vor'ge Ruh' ihr geben kann.

ERSTE DAME
So geht und sagt es ihr,
ich bleib' indessen hier.

ZWEITE DAME
Nein, nein, geht ihr nur hin;
ich wache hier für ihn!

DRITTE DAME
Nein, nein, das kann nicht sein;
ich schütze ihn allein.

ERSTE DAME
Ich bleib' indessen hier.

ZWEITE DAME
Ich wache hier für ihn!

DRITTE DAME
Ich schütze ihn allein!

ERSTE DAME
Ich bleibe!

ZWEITE DAME
Ich wache!

DRITTE DAME
Ich schütze!

ALLE DREI
Ich, ich, ich!

THIRD LADY
Yes, yes! Handsome enough to paint.

ALL THREE
If I were to devote my heart to love,
it would have to be for this young man.
Let us hurry to our Queen
and give this news to her.
It may be that this handsome man
can restore her former peace of mind.

FIRST LADY
Then go and tell her!
Meanwhile I'll stay here.

SECOND LADY
No, no, you just go;
I'll stand guard here.

THIRD LADY
No, no, that cannot be!
I'll protect him alone.

FIRST LADY
Meanwhile I'll stay here.

SECOND LADY
I'll stand guard here!

THIRD LADY
I'll protect him alone!

FIRST LADY
I'll stay!

SECOND LADY
I'll stand guard!

THIRD LADY
I'll protect!

ALLTHREE
I! I! I!

(jede für sich)

Ich sollte fort! Ei, ei, wie fein!
Sie wären gern bei ihm allein.
Nein, nein, das kann nicht sein!

(eine nach der andern, dann alle drei zugleich)

Was wollte ich darum nicht geben,
könnt' ich mit diesem Jüngling leben!
Hätt' ich ihn doch so ganz allein!
Doch keine geht; es kann nicht sein.
Am besten ist es nun, ich geh'.
Du Jüngling, schön und liebevoll,
du trauter Jüngling, lebe wohl,
bis ich dich wieder seh'.

(Sie gehen alle drei zur Pforte des Tempels ab, die sich selbst öffnet und schließt.)

TAMINO *(erwacht, sieht furchtsam umher)*
Wo bin ich! Ist's Fantasie, dass ich noch lebe? Oder hat eine höhere Macht mich gerettet?

(steht auf, sieht umher)

Wie? – Die bösartige Schlange liegt tot zu meinen Füßen?

(Man hört von fern ein Waldflötchen, worunter das Orchester piano accompagniert. Tamino spricht unter dem Ritornell.)

Was hör' ich? Wo bin ich? Welch' unbekannter Ort! Ha, eine männliche Figur nähert sich dem Tal.

(versteckt sich hinter einem Baum)

Zweiter Auftritt

Papageno kommt den Fußsteig herunter, hat auf dem Rücken eine große Vogelsteige, die hoch über den Kopf geht, worin verschiedene Vögel sind; auch hält er mit beiden Händen ein Faunen-Flötchen, pfeift und singt.

(each one aside)

> Am I meant to go? Oh, that's sly!
> They'd like to be alone with him.
> No, no! That cannot be.

(one after the other, then all three together)

> There's nothing I wouldn't give
> to be able to spend my life with this young man!
> If only I had him to myself!
> But no one is leaving; it cannot be.
> It's best now if I go.
> Handsome, adorable young man,
> charming young man, farewell,
> until I see you again.

(All three go down to the temple door, which opens and then closes by itself.)

TAMINO *(wakes, and looks round anxiously)*
> Where am I? Am I just imagining that I'm still alive? Or has some higher power rescued me?

(He stands up, looks around.)

> What? Is the ferocious serpent lying dead at my feet?

(In the distance the sound of pan pipes can be heard, with the orchestra accompanying softly. Tamino speaks during the ritornello.)

> What's that I hear? Where am I? What an unfamiliar place! Ah, that looks like a man coming into the valley.

(hides behind a tree)

Scene 2

Papageno comes down the footpath, with a huge bird crate on his back reaching up high above his head; inside are various birds; he is also holding pan pipes in both hands, playing and singing.

75

Nr. 2 Arie

PAPAGENO

Der Vogelfänger bin ich ja,   [2]
stets lustig, heißa, hopsasa!
Der Vogelfänger ist bekannt
bei Alt und Jung im ganzen Land.
Weiß mit dem Locken umzugehn,
und mich aufs Pfeifen zu verstehn.
Drum kann ich froh und lustig sein,
denn alle Vögel sind ja mein.

(pfeift)

Der Vogelfänger bin ich ja,
stets lustig, heißa! hopsasa!
Der Vogelfänger ist bekannt
bei Alt und Jung im ganzen Land.
Ein Netz für Mädchen möchte ich,
ich fing' sie dutzendweis' für mich.
Dann sperrte ich sie bei mir ein,
und alle Mädchen wären mein.

(pfeift)

Wenn alle Mädchen wären mein,
so tauschte ich brav Zucker ein:
die, welche mir am liebsten wär',
der gäb' ich gleich den Zucker her.
Und küsste sie mich zärtlich dann,
wär' sie mein Weib und ich ihr Mann.
Sie schlief' an meiner Seite ein,
ich wiegte wie ein Kind sie ein.

(pfeift, will nach der Arie nach der Pforte gehen)

TAMINO *(nimmt ihn bei der Hand)*
He da!

PAPAGENO
Was da?

76

No. 2 Aria

PAPAGENO
    I'm the birdcatcher,   [2]
    always cheerful, hip hurrah!
    The birdcatcher is known
    to old and young throughout the land.
    I know how to set a trap,
    and whistle so the birds know what I'm saying.
    That's why I can be happy and cheerful,
    for all the birds belong to me.

(plays)

    I'm the birdcatcher,
    always cheerful, hip hurrah!
    The birdcatcher is known
    to old and young throughout the land.
    I'd like to have a net for girls;
    I'd catch myself them by the dozen.
    I'd keep them by me in a cage,
    and all the girls would belong to me.

(plays)

If all the girls belonged to me,
I'd trade for some nice sugar,
and I'd instantly give the sugar
to the girl I liked the most.
And she'd then kiss me tenderly,
if she were my wife, and I her husband.
She'd fall asleep beside me.
and I'd rock her like a child.

This verse does not appear in the 1791 score or libretto. See p. 28, note 5.

(plays, and after the aria goes towards the door)

TAMINO *(takes his hand)*
    Hey there!

PAPAGENO
    What there?

TAMINO
Sag mir, du lustiger Freund, wer du seist.

PAPAGENO
Wer ich bin?

(für sich)

Dumme Frage!

(laut)

Ein Mensch, wie du. Wenn ich dich nun fragte, wer du bist?

TAMINO
So würde ich dir antworten, dass ich aus fürstlichem Geblüte bin.

PAPAGENO
Das ist mir zu hoch. Musst dich deutlicher erklären, wenn ich dich verstehen soll!

TAMINO
Mein Vater ist Fürst, der über viele Länder und Menschen herrscht; darum nennt man mich Prinz.

PAPAGENO
Länder? Menschen? Prinz?

TAMINO
Daher frag' ich dich!

PAPAGENO
Langsam! Lass mich fragen. Sag du mir zuvor: gibt's außer diesen Bergen auch noch Länder und Menschen?

TAMINO
Viele Tausende!

PAPAGENO
Da ließ' sich eine Spekulation mit meinen Vögeln machen.

TAMINO
Nun sag du mir, in welcher Gegend wir sind.

TAMINO
Tell me, my cheerful friend, who might you be?

PAPAGENO
Who am I?

(*aside*)

Stupid question!

(*aloud*)

A human being, like you. If I now asked you who you are?

TAMINO
Then I'd answer that I am of princely blood.

PAPAGENO
That's too far above me. You'll have to express yourself more clearly if I'm to understand you!

TAMINO
My father is a king who rules over many lands and people; so I am called Prince.

PAPAGENO
Lands? People? Prince?

TAMINO
That's why I'm asking!

PAPAGENO
Not so fast! Let me ask. First tell me: are there more lands and people beyond these mountains, then?

TAMINO
Many thousands!

PAPAGENO
Then I can do some business with my birds.

TAMINO
Now, tell me whereabouts we are.

PAPAGENO
In welcher Gegend?

(sieht sich um)

Zwischen Tälern und Bergen.

TAMINO
Schon recht! Aber wie nennt man eigentlich diese Gegend? Wer beherrscht sie?

PAPAGENO
Das kann ich dir ebensowenig beantworten, als ich weiß, wie ich auf die Welt gekommen bin.

TAMINO *(lacht)*
Wie? Du wüsstest nicht, wo du geboren, oder wer deine Eltern waren?

PAPAGENO
Kein Wort! Ich weiß nicht mehr und nicht weniger, als dass mich ein alter, aber sehr lustiger Mann auferzogen und ernährt hat.

TAMINO
Das war vermutlich dein Vater?

PAPAGENO
Das weiß ich nicht.

TAMINO
Hattest du denn deine Mutter nicht gekannt?

PAPAGENO
Gekannt hab' ich sie nicht; erzählen ließ ich mir's einige Mal, dass meine Mutter einst da in diesem verschlossenen Gebäude bei der nächtlich sternflammenden Königin gedient hätte. Ob sie noch lebt, oder was aus ihr geworden ist, weiß ich nicht. Ich weiß nur so viel, dass nicht weit von hier meine Strohhütte steht, die mich vor Regen und Kälte schützt.

TAMINO
Aber wie lebst du?

PAPAGENO
    Whereabouts?

(looks around)

    Between valleys and mountains.

TAMINO
    Indeed! But what is name of this place?
    Who is its ruler?

PAPAGENO
    I can no more answer you that than tell you how I came into this
    world.

TAMINO *(laughs)*
    What? Don't you know where you were born, or who your
    parents were?

PAPAGENO
    No idea! I know no more and no less than that a jolly old man
    brought me up and fed me.

TAMINO
    That was probably your father?

PAPAGENO
    I don't know.

TAMINO
    So did you not know your mother?

PAPAGENO
    I didn't know her; someone once told me that my mother used
    to serve the blazing star queen in this closed building. Whether
    she's still alive, or what became of her, I've no idea. All I know
    is that not far from here is my straw hut, which shelters me from
    rain and cold.

TAMINO
    But how do you live?

PAPAGENO
Von Essen und Trinken, wie alle Menschen.

TAMINO
Wodurch erhältst du das?

PAPAGENO
Durch Tausch. Ich fange für die sternflammende Königin und ihre Jungfrauen verschiedene Vögel; dafür erhalt' ich täglich Speis' und Trank von ihr.

TAMINO *(für sich)*
Sternflammende Königin! Wenn es etwa gar die mächtige Herrscherin der Nacht wäre! Sag mir, guter Freund! Warst du schon so glücklich, diese Göttin der Nacht zu sehen?

PAPAGENO *(der bisher öfters auf seiner Flöte geblasen)*
Deine letzte alberne Frage überzeugt mich, dass du aus einem fremden Land geboren bist.

TAMINO
Sei darüber nicht ungehalten, lieber Freund! Ich dachte nur—

PAPAGENO
Die sternflammende Königin sehen? Wenn du noch mit einer solchen albernen Frage an mich kommst, so sperr' ich dich, so wahr ich Papageno heiße, wie einen Gimpel in mein Vogelhaus, verhandle dich dann mit meinen übrigen Vögeln an die nächtliche Königin und ihre Jungfrauen, dann mögen sie dich meinetwegen sieden oder braten.

TAMINO *(für sich)*
Ein wunderlicher Mann!

PAPAGENO
Die sternflammende Königin sehen? Welcher Sterbliche kann sich rühmen, sie je gesehen zu haben? Welches Menschen Auge würde durch ihren schwarz durchwebten Schleier blicken können?

TAMINO *(für sich)*
Nun ist's klar; es ist eben diese nächtliche Königin, von der mein Vater mir so oft erzählte. Aber zu fassen, wie ich mich hierher verirrte,

PAPAGENO

By eating and drinking, like everybody else.

TAMINO

How do you obtain that?

PAPAGENO

By barter. I catch all kinds of birds for the blazing star queen and her young ladies; every day I get food and drink for them from her.

TAMINO (*aside*)

Blazing star queen! I wonder if that could be the mighty Queen of the Night! Tell me, my good friend, have you ever been fortunate enough to see this goddess of the night?

PAPAGENO (*who has been repeatedly playing his pipes*)

Your last stupid question convinces me that you were born in another country.

TAMINO

Don't get so annoyed, my dear friend! I merely thought—

PAPAGENO

See the blazing star queen? If you come to me again with as stupid a question as that, I'll lock you up in my birdhouse like a bullfinch, as sure as my name's Papageno, then I'll sell you along with my other birds to the Queen of the Night and her young ladies, and then I hope they boil or roast you.

TAMINO (*aside*)

What an extraordinary man!

PAPAGENO

See the blazing star queen? What mortal can claim ever to have seen her? What human eye would be able to look through her black, woven veil?

TAMINO (*aside*)

It's clear now: this is the very Queen of the Night that my father told me about so often. But it's beyond me how I ended

ist außer meiner Macht. Unfehlbar ist auch dieser Mann kein gewöhnlicher Mensch. Vielleicht einer ihrer dienstbaren Geister.

PAPAGENO *(für sich)*

Wie er mich so starr anblickt! Bald fang' ich an, mich vor ihm zu fürchten. Warum siehst du so verdächtig und schelmisch nach mir?

TAMINO

Weil – weil ich zweifle, ob du Mensch bist.

PAPAGENO

Wie war das?

TAMINO

Nach deinen Federn, die dich bedecken, halt' ich dich—

(geht auf ihn zu)

PAPAGENO

Doch für keinen Vogel? – Bleib zurück, sag' ich, und traue mir nicht; denn ich habe Riesenkraft, wenn ich jemand packe.

(für sich)

Wenn er sich nicht bald von mir schrecken lässt, so lauf' ich davon.

TAMINO

Riesenkraft?

(Er sieht auf die Schlange.)

Also warst du wohl gar mein Erretter, der diese giftige Schlange bekämpfte?

PAPAGENO

Schlange!

(sieht sich um, weicht zitternd einige Schritte zurück)

Was da! Ist sie tot, oder lebendig?

up in this place. And this man too is certainly no ordinary person. Perhaps one of her attendant spirits.

PAPAGENO *(aside)*
How he's staring straight at me! He's going to scare me soon. Why are you giving me such suspicious, roguish looks?

TAMINO
Because – because I'm not sure if you're a human.

PAPAGENO
What?

TAMINO
From the feathers that cover you, I'd say you were—

(approaches him)

PAPAGENO
Not a bird, surely? Stand back, I say, and beware, for I have the strength of a giant when I get hold of someone.

(aside)

If I can't quickly frighten him, I'll run away.

TAMINO
Strength of a giant?

(He looks at the serpent.)

So I take it you were my saviour who tackled this poisonous serpent?

PAPAGENO
Serpent!

(looks around, takes a few steps back in fright)

Goodness! Is it dead or alive?

TAMINO

Du willst durch deine bescheidene Frage meinen Dank ablehnen – aber ich muss dir sagen, dass ich ewig für deine so tapfere Handlung dankbar sein werde.

PAPAGENO

Schweigen wir davon still – freuen wir uns, dass sie glücklich überwunden ist.

TAMINO

Aber um alles in der Welt, Freund! Wie hast du dieses Ungeheuer bekämpft? Du bist ohne Waffen.

PAPAGENO

Brauch' keine! Bei mir ist ein starker Druck mit der Hand mehr, als Waffen.

TAMINO

Du hast sie also erdrosselt?

PAPAGENO

Erdrosselt!

(*für sich*)

Bin in meinem Leben nicht so stark gewesen, als heute.

Dritter Auftritt

Die Vorigen, die drei Damen

DIE DREI DAMEN *(drohen und rufen zugleich)*
Papageno!

PAPAGENO

Aha! Das geht mich an. Sieh dich um, Freund!

TAMINO

Wer sind diese Damen?

TAMINO

You ask that question to modestly rebuff my thanks – but I have to tell you that I shall be eternally grateful for your fearless deed.

PAPAGENO

Let's not talk about that. Let's just be glad that fortunately it's been overpowered.

TAMINO

But, my friend, how on earth did you tackle this monster? You don't have any weapons.

PAPAGENO

Don't need any! A tight squeeze of my hand is more effective than a weapon.

TAMINO

Did you strangle it, then?

PAPAGENO

Strangled!

(aside)

I've never in my life been so strong as I am today.

Scene 3

The above, the Three Ladies

THE THREE LADIES *(calling menacingly all together)*
Papageno!

PAPAGENO

Aha! That's for me. Look round, my friend!

TAMINO

Who are these ladies?

PAPAGENO

Wer sie eigentlich sind, weiß ich selbst nicht. Ich weiß nur so viel, dass sie mir täglich meine Vögel abnehmen und mir dafür Wein, Zuckerbrot und süße Feigen bringen.

TAMINO

Sie sind vermutlich sehr schön?

PAPAGENO

Ich denke nicht! – denn wenn sie schön wären, würden sie ihre Gesichter nicht bedecken.

DIE DREI DAMEN (*drohend*)

Papageno!

PAPAGENO

Sei still! Sie drohen mir schon. Du fragst, ob sie schön sind, und ich kann dir darauf nichts antworten, als dass ich in meinem Leben nichts Reizenderes sah.

(*für sich*)

Jetzt werden sie bald wieder gut werden.

DIE DREI DAMEN (*drohend*)

Papageno!

PAPAGENO

Was muss ich denn heute verbrochen haben, dass sie gar so aufgebracht wider mich sind? – Hier, meine Schönen, übergeb' ich meine Vögel.

ERSTE DAME (*reicht ihm eine schöne Bouteille Wasser*)

Dafür schickt dir unsre Fürstin heute zum ersten Mal statt Wein reines helles Wasser.

ZWEITE DAME

Und mir befahl sie, dass ich, statt Zuckerbrot, diesen Stein dir überbringen soll. Ich wünsche, dass er dir wohl bekommen möge.

PAPAGENO

Was? Steine soll ich fressen?

PAPAGENO
> Who they actually are I don't know myself. All I know is that every day they take my birds and bring me wine, cake and sweet figs for them.

TAMINO
> Can I assume they're very beautiful?

PAPAGENO
> I don't think so! If they were beautiful they wouldn't cover their faces.

THE THREE LADIES *(threateningly)*
> Papageno!

PAPAGENO
> Quiet! Now they're threatening me. You ask if they're beautiful, and the only answer I can give is that I have never seen anything lovelier in my life.

(aside)

> Now they'll soon be nice again.

THE THREE LADIES *(threateningly)*
> Papageno!

PAPAGENO
> What can I have done wrong today to make them so angry with me? – Here, lovely ladies, are my birds for you.

FIRST LADY *(hands him an attractive water bottle)*
> For that today our Queen sends you for the first time instead of wine, pure, clear water.

SECOND LADY
> And she commanded me to give you, instead of cake, this stone. I hope you like it.

PAPAGENO
> What? Am I meant to eat stones?

DRITTE DAME

Und statt der süßen Feigen hab' ich die Ehre, dir dies goldene Schloss vor den Mund zu schlagen.

(Sie schlägt ihm das Schloss vor.)

(Papageno zeigt seinen Scherz durch Gebärden.)

ERSTE DAME

Du willst vermutlich wissen, warum die Fürstin dich heute so wunderbar bestraft?

(Papageno bejaht es.)

ZWEITE DAME

Damit du künftig nie mehr Fremde belügst.

DRITTE DAME

Und dass du nie dich der Heldentaten rühmst, die andre vollzogen.

ERSTE DAME

Sag' an! Hast du diese Schlange bekämpft?

(Papageno deutet nein.)

ZWEITE DAME

Wer denn also?

(Papageno deutet, er wisse es nicht.)

DRITTE DAME

Wir waren's, Jüngling, die dich befreiten. Zittre nicht! Dich erwartet Freude und Entzücken. Hier, dies Gemälde schickt dir die große Fürstin; es ist das Bildnis ihrer Tochter – findest du, sagte sie, dass diese Züge dir nicht gleichgültig sind, dann ist Glück, Ehr' und Ruhm dein Los. Auf Wiedersehen.

(geht ab)

ZWEITE DAME

Adieu, Monsieur Papageno!

(geht ab)

THIRD LADY
> And, instead of sweet figs, I have the honour of fixing this golden lock on your mouth.

(She puts the lock on him.)

(Papageno gestures to demonstrate his pain.)

FIRST LADY
> I suspect you want to know why the Queen is giving you such a prodigious punishment today?

(Papageno nods.)

SECOND LADY
> So that in future you don't lie to strangers.

THIRD LADY
> And so that you never boast of heroic deeds carried out by others.

FIRST LADY
> Speak up! Did you fight this serpent?

(Papageno shakes his head.)

SECOND LADY
> So who did?

(Papageno signals that he doesn't know.)

THIRD LADY
> It was we, young man, who rescued you. Do not be afraid! Joy and delight await you. Here, the great Queen sends you this painting; it is the portrait of her daughter. If, she says, you are not indifferent to these features, then happiness, honour and fame await you. Farewell.

(exit)

SECOND LADY
> Adieu, Monsieur Papageno!

(exit)

ERSTE DAME
Fein nicht zu hastig getrunken!

(geht lachend ab)

(Papageno hat immer sein stummes Spiel gehabt. Tamino ist gleich bei Empfang des Bildnisses aufmerksam geworden; seine Liebe nimmt zu, ob er gleich für alle diese Reden taub schien.)

Vierter Auftritt

Tamino, Papageno.

Nr. 3 Arie

TAMINO
Dies Bildnis ist bezaubernd schön,   [3]
wie noch kein Auge je gesehn.
Ich fühl' es, wie dies Götterbild
mein Herz mit neuer Regung füllt.

Dies Etwas kann ich zwar nicht nennen.
Doch fühl' ich hier wie Feuer brennen.
Soll die Empfindung Liebe sein?
Ja, ja! die Liebe ist's allein.

O wenn ich sie nur finden könnte!
O wenn sie doch schon vor mir stände!
Ich würde – würde – warm und rein –

Was würde ich? – Ich würde sie voll Entzücken
an diesen heißen Busen drücken,
und ewig wäre sie dann mein.

(will ab)

Fünfter Auftritt

Vorige, die drei Damen

ERSTE DAME
Rüste dich mit Mut und Standhaftigkeit, schöner Jüngling! Die
Fürstin—

FIRST LADY
Don't drink too quickly!

(exit, laughing)

(Papageno has kept up his silent mime. Tamino has been absorbed since receiving the portrait; he is falling in love, although he seemed struck dumb through all the dialogue.)

Scene 4

Tamino, Papageno.

No. 3 Aria

TAMINO
This portrait is enchantingly beautiful,   [3]
such as no eye has ever seen!
I feel this heavenly picture
stirring something new in my heart.

I cannot give a name to what this is!
Yet I feel it here burning like a fire.
Can this sensation be love?
Yes! It is love, and nothing else.

Oh, if only I could find her!
Oh, if she were already standing before me!
I would – would – with pure devotion –

What would I do? – In rapture
I would press her to my burning breast,
and then she would be mine for ever.

(makes to leave)

Scene 5

The above, the Three Ladies.

FIRST LADY
Arm yourself with courage and fortitude, young man! The Queen—

ZWEITE DAME
hat mir aufgetragen, dir zu sagen—

DRITTE DAME
dass der Weg zu deinem künftigen Glücke nunmehr gebahnt sei.

ERSTE DAME
Sie hat jedes deiner Worte gehört, so du sprachst; sie hat—

ZWEITE DAME
jeden Zug in deinem Gesichte gelesen. Ja noch mehr, ihr mütterliches Herz—

DRITTE DAME
hat beschlossen, dich ganz glücklich zu machen. – Hat dieser Jüngling, sprach sie, auch so viel Mut und Tapferkeit, als er zärtlich ist, o so ist meine Tochter ganz gewiss gerettet.

TAMINO
Gerettet? O ewige Dunkelheit! Was hör' ich? Das Original?—

ERSTE DAME
hat ein mächtiger, böser Dämon ihr entrissen.

TAMINO
Entrissen? O ihr Götter! – sagt, wie konnte das geschehen?

ERSTE DAME
Sie saß an einem schönen Maientage ganz allein in dem alles belebenden Zypressenwäldchen, welches immer ihr Lieblingsaufenthalt war. Der Bösewicht schlich unbemerkt hinein—

ZWEITE DAME
belauschte sie, und—

DRITTE DAME
er hat nebst seinem bösen Herzen auch noch die Macht, sich in jede erdenkliche Gestalt zu verwandeln; auf solche Weise hat er auch Pamina—

ERSTE DAME
Dies ist der Name der königlichen Tochter, so Ihr anbetet.

SECOND LADY
has bade me tell you—

THIRD LADY
that the way to your future happiness is no longer closed to you.

FIRST LADY
She has heard every word you spoke; she has—

SECOND LADY
read every feature on your face. Even more, her motherly heart—

THIRD LADY
has decided to make you completely happy. If this young man, she said, is as courageous and daring as he is tender, then my daughter will surely be rescued.

TAMINO
Rescued? O eternal darkness! What am I hearing? The original?—

FIRST LADY
was snatched from her by a powerful, evil demon.

TAMINO
Snatched? O you gods! Tell me, how could that happen?

FIRST LADY
One lovely day in May she was sitting all alone in the cool cypress grove, which has always been her favourite place. The villain crept in unseen—

SECOND LADY
listened to her, and—

THIRD LADY
as well as his evil heart, he also has the power to take on every imaginable form; this is how Pamina too—

FIRST LADY
This is the name of the Queen's daughter, whom you adore.

TAMINO

O Pamina! Du mir entrissen – du in der Gewalt eines üppigen Bösewichts! – Bist vielleicht in diesem Augenblicke – schrecklicher Gedanke!

DIE DREI DAMEN

Schweig, Jüngling!

ERSTE DAME

Lästere der holden Schönheit Tugend nicht! Trotz aller Pein, so die Unschuld duldet, ist sie sich immer gleich. Weder Zwang, noch Schmeichelei ist vermögend, sie zum Wege des Lasters zu verführen.

TAMINO

O sagt, Mädchen! Sagt, wo ist des Tyrannen Aufenthalt?

ZWEITE DAME

Sehr nahe an unsern Bergen lebt er in einem angenehmen und reizenden Tale. Seine Burg ist prachtvoll, und sorgsam bewacht.

TAMINO

Kommt, Mädchen! führt mich! Pamina sei gerettet! Der Bösewicht falle von meinem Arm; das schwör ich bei meiner Liebe, bei meinem Herzen!

(Sogleich wird ein heftig erschütternder Akkord mit Musik gehört.)

Ihr Götter! Was ist das?

DIE DREI DAMEN

Fasse dich!

ERSTE DAME

Es verkündigt die Ankunft unserer Königin.

(Donner)

DIE DREI DAMEN

Sie kommt!

(Donner)

Sie kommt!

TAMINO

O Pamina! Snatched from me – in the power of a wanton villain! Perhaps at this very moment – what a dreadful thought!

THE THREE LADIES

Hush, young man!

FIRST LADY

Do not besmirch the noble beauty's virtue! Despite all the pain that she innocently suffers, she is still as she was. Neither force nor wheedling was able to tempt her on to the path of vice.

TAMINO

Tell me, young ladies, where does the tyrant live?

SECOND LADY

He lives in a pleasant, beautiful valley very close to our mountains. His magnificent fortress is closely guarded.

TAMINO

Come, ladies, lead me! Pamina will be rescued! Let me bring down the villain; I swear I shall, by my love and by my heart!

(A powerful, terrifying chord is immediately heard.)

You gods! What is that?

THE THREE LADIES

Do not be afraid!

FIRST LADY

It heralds the arrival of our Queen.

(thunder)

THE THREE LADIES

She comes!

(thunder)

She comes!

(Donner)

Sie kommt!

(Donner)

Sechster Auftritt

Die Berge teilen sich auseinander, und das Theater verwandelt sich in ein prächtiges Gemach.

Die Königin der Nacht sitzt auf einem Thron, welcher mit transparenten Sternen geziert ist. [4a]

Nr. 4 Rezitativ und Arie

KÖNIGIN DER NACHT

O zittre nicht, mein lieber Sohn! [4b]
Du bist unschuldig, weise, fromm.
Ein Jüngling, so wie du, vermag am besten,
dies tief betrübte Mutterherz zu trösten.

Zum Leiden bin ich auserkoren, [4c]
denn meine Tochter fehlet mir.
Durch sie ging all mein Glück verloren,
ein Bösewicht entfloh mit ihr.
Noch seh' ich ihr Zittern
mit bangem Erschüttern,
ihr ängstliches Beben,
ihr schüchternes Streben.
Ich musste sie mir rauben sehen.
Ach helft! War alles was sie sprach;
allein vergebens war ihr Flehen,
denn meine Hilfe war zu schwach.

Du wirst sie zu befreien gehen,
du wirst der Tochter Retter sein. Ja!
Und werd ich dich als Sieger sehen,
so sei sie dann auf ewig dein.

(mit den drei Damen ab)

(thunder)

She comes!

(thunder)

Scene 6

The mountains split apart, and the scene changes to a lavish chamber.

The Queen of the Night is seated on a throne decorated with transparent stars.   [4a]

No. 4 Recitative and Aria

QUEEN OF THE NIGHT
O do not be afraid, my dear son!   [4b]
You are innocent, upright, wise;
a young man such as you can best console
a mother's grief-stricken heart.

I am condemned to grief;   [4c]
for my daughter has gone.
All my happiness was lost with her:
an evil man spirited her away.
I can still see her trembling
with fear and shock,
her anxious shaking,
her desperate struggling.
I was forced to witness her being taken,
'Ah, help me!' was all she said:
but her pleanding was in vain,
for I was too weak to help.

You will go and free her,
you will be my daughter's saviour. Yes!
And when I see you victorious,
then she will be yours for ever.

(exit with the Three Ladies)

99

Siebenter Auftritt

Tamino, Papageno.

Das Theater verwandelt sich wieder so, wie es vorher war.

TAMINO *(nach einer Pause)*
Ist's denn auch Wirklichkeit, was ich sah? Oder betäubten mich meine Sinnen? O ihr guten Götter, täuscht mich nicht! Oder ich unterliege eurer Prüfung. Schützet meinen Arm, stählt meinen Mut, und Taminos Herz wird ewigen Dank euch entgegenschlagen.

(Er will gehen, Papageno tritt ihm in den Weg.)

Nr. 5 Quintett

PAPAGENO *(mit dem Schlosse vor dem Maul, winkt darauf)*
Hm! Hm! Hm! Hm! Hm! Hm! Hm! Hm!   [5a]

TAMINO
Der Arme kann von Strafe sagen,
denn seine Sprache ist dahin.

PAPAGENO
Hm! Hm! Hm! Hm! Hm! Hm! Hm! Hm!

TAMINO
Ich kann nichts tun, als dich beklagen,
weil ich zu schwach zu helfen bin.

PAPAGENO
Hm! Hm! Hm! Hm! Hm! Hm! Hm! Hm!

Achter Auftritt

Vorige, die drei Damen

ERSTE DAME
Die Königin begnadigt dich!

(nimmt ihm das Schloss vom Maul weg)

Entlässt die Strafe dir durch mich.

100

Scene 7

Tamino, Papageno.

The scene turns back to the way it was before.

TAMINO *(after a pause)*
    Did I really see that? Or are my senses stunned? O kindly gods,
    do not deceive me, or I shall fail your test. Protect my arm,
    steel my courage, and Tamino's heart will be eternally grateful
    to you.

(He starts to leave, but Papageno blocks his way.)

No. 5 Quintet

PAPAGENO *(dejectedly pointing to the lock on his mouth)*
    Hm! Hm! Hm! Hm! Hm! Hm! Hm! Hm!   [5a]

TAMINO
    The poor fellow has certainly been punished,
    he cannot speak a word.

PAPAGENO
    Hm! Hm! Hm! Hm! Hm! Hm! Hm! Hm!

TAMINO
    All I can do is offer sympathy,
    for I am powerless to help.

PAPAGENO
    Hm! Hm! Hm! Hm! Hm! Hm! Hm! Hm!

Scene 8

The above, the Three Ladies.

FIRST LADY
    The Queen pardons you!

(removes the lock from his mouth)

    Through me she relieves your punishment.

101

PAPAGENO
  Nun plaudert Papageno wieder!

ZWEITE DAME
  Ja plaudre – lüge nur nicht wieder.

PAPAGENO
  Ich lüge nimmermehr! Nein! Nein!

DIE DREI DAMEN und PAPAGENO
  Dies Schloss soll deine/meine Warnung sein!

ALLE FÜNF
  Bekämen doch die Lügner alle
  ein solches Schloss vor ihren Mund:
  statt Hass, Verleumdung, schwarzer Galle,
  bestünde Lieb und Bruderbund.

ERSTE DAME
  O Prinz, nimm dies Geschenk von mir!
  Dies sendet unsre Fürstin dir.

(*gibt ihm eine goldene Flöte*)

  Die Zauberflöte wird dich schützen,
  im grössten Unglück unterstützen.

DIE DREI DAMEN
  Hiermit kannst du allmächtig handeln,
  der Menschen Leidenschaft verwandeln.
  Der Traurige wird freudig sein,
  den Hagestolz nimmt Liebe ein.

ALLE FÜNF
  O so eine Flöte ist mehr
  als Gold und Kronen wert,
  denn durch sie wird Menschenglück
  und Zufriedenheit vermehrt.

PAPAGENO
  Nun, ihr schönen Frauenzimmer,
  darf ich? So empfehl ich mich?

PAPAGENO
Can Papageno now chatter again?

SECOND LADY
Chatter away! Just don't lie again.

PAPAGENO
I'll never tell a lie again! No, no!

THE THREE LADIES and PAPAGENO
Let this lock be a warning to you/me.

ALL FIVE
If all liars were given
such a lock for their mouths,
hatred and slander, black anger
would be replaced by love and friendship.

FIRST LADY
O Prince, accept this present from me!
Our Queen sends this to you!

(gives him a golden flute)

The magic flute will protect you
and support you in the worst misfortune.

THE THREE LADIES
With this you will be all-powerful
and change men's hearts.
The downcast will rejoice,
the loveless will love.

ALL FIVE
Such a flute
is worth more than gold and crowns,
for through it mankind's happiness
and contentment will grow

PAPAGENO
Now, you fair ladies,
may I then take my leave?

DIE DREI DAMEN
Dich empfehlen kannst du immer,
doch bestimmt die Fürstin dich,
mit dem Prinzen ohn' Verweilen
nach Sarastros Burg zu eilen.

PAPAGENO
Nein, dafür bedank ich mich.
Von euch selbst hörte ich,
dass er wie ein Tigertier,
sicher ließ ohn' alle Gnaden
mich Sarastro rupfen, braten,
setzte mich den Hunden für.

DIE DREI DAMEN
Dich schützt der Prinz, trau ihm allein,
dafür sollst du sein Diener sein.

PAPAGENO *(für sich)*
Dass doch der Prinz beim Teufel wäre,
mein Leben ist mir lieb.
Am Ende schleicht bei meiner Ehre,
er von mir wie ein Dieb.

ERSTE DAME
Hier nimm dies Kleinod, es ist dein.

(gibt ihm eine Maschine wie ein stahlnes Gelächter [Glockenspiel])

PAPAGENO
Ei! Ei! was mag darinnen sein?

DRITTE DAME
Darinnen hörst du Glöckchen tönen!

PAPAGENO
Werd ich sie auch wohl spielen können?

DIE DREI DAMEN
O ganz gewiss! Ja, ja, gewiss!

THE THREE LADIES
> You can take your leave,
> but the Queen has decided
> that you must hurry without delay
> to Sarastro's castle with the Prince.

PAPAGENO
> No, thank you!
> I've heard from you yourselves
> that he is like a tiger,
> Sarastro will surely mercilessly
> have me plucked and roasted,
> and feed me to his dogs.

THE THREE LADIES
> The Prince will protect you; trust in him alone.
> That's why you must serve him.

PAPAGENO *(aside)*
> The Prince can go to the devil;
> I'm fond of my life.
> I'll bet anything he'll end up
> sneaking away from me like a thief.

FIRST LADY
> Take this treasure – it's for you.

(gives him a contraption that looks like a steel glockenspiel)

PAPAGENO
> Well, well! What could be inside?

THIRD LADY
> You'll hear little bells ringing inside.

PAPAGENO
> Might I be able to play them too?

THE THREE LADIES
> Oh yes, of course! Yes, of course!

ALLE FÜNF
Silberglöckchen, Zauberflöten
sind zu eurem/unserm Schutz vonnöten!
Lebet wohl! Wir wollen gehn!
Lebet wohl! – Auf Wiedersehen.

(Alle wollen gehen.)

TAMINO
Doch schöne Damen saget an…

PAPAGENO
…wo man die Burg wohl finden kann?

DIE DREI DAMEN
Drei Knäbchen, jung, schön, hold und weise,   [5b]
umschweben euch auf eurer Reise.
Sie werden eure Führer sein,
folgt ihrem Rate ganz allein.

TAMINO und PAPAGENO
Drei Knäbchen jung, schön, hold und weise,
umschweben uns auf unsrer Reise.

ALLE FÜNF
So lebet wohl! Wir wollen gehen,
lebt wohl, lebt wohl, auf Wiedersehen!

(Alle ab.)

Neunter Auftritt

Zwei Sklaven tragen, so bald das Theater in ein prächtiges ägyptisches Zimmer verwandelt ist, schöne Polster nebst einem prächtigen türkischen Tisch heraus, breiten Teppiche auf, sodann kommt der dritte Sklave.

DRITTER SKLAVE
Ha, ha, ha!

ERSTER SKLAVE
Pst, Pst!

ALL FIVE
Silver bells, magic flutes,
are needed for your/our protection.
Farewell – we shall go.
Farewell, till we meet again.

(All are about to go.)

TAMINO
But say, fair ladies …

PAPAGENO
…where we can find the castle?

THE THREE LADIES
Three boys, young, handsome, meek and wise,   [5b]
will hover around you on your journey.
They will be your guides –
follow only their advice.

TAMINO and PAPAGENO
Three boys, young, handsome, meek and wise,
will hover around us on our journey.

ALL FIVE
Farewell, we shall go,
farewell, farewell, till we meet again!

(All leave.)

Scene 9

*As soon as the scene has changed to a sumptuous Egyptian room,
two slaves carry on beautiful cushions and a splendid Turkish table
and lay out broad carpets, and then the third slave appears.*

THIRD SLAVE
Ha, ha, ha!

FIRST SLAVE
Pst, Pst!

ZWEITER SKLAVE
Was soll denn das Lachen?

DRITTER SKLAVE
Unser Peiniger, der alles belauschende Mohr, wird morgen sicherlich gehangen oder gespießt. Pamina! Ha, ha, ha!

ERSTER SKLAVE
Nun?

DRITTE SKLAVE
Das reizende Mädchen! Ha, ha, ha!

ZWEITER SKLAVE
Nun?

DRITTER SKLAVE
Ist entsprungen.

ERSTER und ZWEITER SKLAVE
Entsprungen?

ERSTER SKLAVE
Und sie entkam?

DRITTE SKLAVE
Unfehlbar! – Wenigstens ist's mein wahrer Wunsch.

ERSTER SKLAVE
O Dank euch, ihr guten Götter! Ihr habt meine Bitte erhört.

DRITTER SKLAVE
Sagt' ich euch nicht immer, es wird doch ein Tag für uns scheinen, wo
wir gerochen, und der schwarze Monostatos bestraft werden wird.

ZWEITER SKLAVE
Was spricht nun der Mohr zu der Geschichte?

ERSTER SKLAVE
Er weiß doch davon?

SECOND SLAVE
What's the laughing about?

THIRD SLAVE
Our tormentor, the Moor who listens to everything, is surely going to be either hanged or impaled tomorrow. Pamina! Ha, ha, ha!

FIRST SLAVE
Well?

THIRD SLAVE
The lovely maiden! Ha, ha, ha!

SECOND SLAVE
What?

THIRD SLAVE
She's run away.

FIRST and SECOND SLAVE
Run away?

FIRST SLAVE
Did she escape?

THIRD SLAVE
Definitely! At least I hope she did.

FIRST SLAVE
Thank the good gods! My prayer has been answered.

THIRD SLAVE
Haven't I always said that the day would finally come for us when we would be avenged, and the black Monostatos punished.

SECOND SLAVE
What does the Moor have to say about this?

FIRST SLAVE
Does he know?

DRITTER SKLAVE
Natürlich! Sie entlief vor seinen Augen. – Wie mir einige Brüder
erzählten, die im Garten arbeiteten, und von weitem sahen und
hörten, so ist der Mohr nicht mehr zu retten; auch wenn Pamina
von Sarastros Gefolge wieder eingebracht würde.

ERSTER und ZWEITER SKLAVE
Wieso?

DRITTER SKLAVE
Du kennst ja den üppigen Wanst und seine Weise; das Mädchen
aber war klüger, als ich dachte. In dem Augenblicke, da er zu
siegen glaubte, rief sie Sarastros Namen: das erschütterte den
Mohren; er blieb stumm und unbeweglich stehen – indes lief
Pamina nach dem Kanal und schiffte von selbst in einer Gondel
dem Palmenwäldchen zu.

ERSTER SKLAVE
O wie wird das schüchterne Reh mit Todesängsten zum Palast
ihrer zärtlichen Mutter zueilen.

Zehnter Auftritt

Vorige, Monostatos von innen.

MONOSTATOS
He Sklaven!

ERSTER SKLAVE
Monostatos' Stimme!

MONOSTATOS
He Sklaven! Schaft Fesseln herbei!

DIE DREI SKLAVEN
Fesseln?

ERSTER SKLAVE *(läuft zur Seitentür)*
Doch nicht für Pamina? Oh, ihr Götter! Da seht, Brüder, das
Mädchen ist gefangen!

ZWEITER und DRITTER SKLAVE
Pamina? – Schrecklicher Anblick!

THIRD SLAVE
Of course! She got away under his very eyes. According to some
of our comrades who were working in the garden and only
saw and heard from a distance, time's up for the Moor, even if
Pamina is caught again by Sarastro's people.

FIRST and SECOND SLAVE
Why's that?

THIRD SLAVE
You know what the potbellied one is like – but the girl was
smarter than I thought. Just as he thought victory was as-
sured, she called out Sarastro's name; that shook the Moor
and he stopped dead in his tracks, struck dumb; then Pamina
ran to the canal and sailed off on a gondola towards the
palm grove.

FIRST SLAVE
Now I'm sure the shy doe is running for her life towards her
tender mother's palace.

Scene 10

The above, Monostatos within.

MONOSTATOS
Hey, slaves!

FIRST SLAVE
That's Monostatos's voice!

MONOSTATOS
Hey, slaves! Fetch the shackles!

THE THREE SLAVES
Shackles?

FIRST SLAVE *(runs to the side door)*
Surely not for Pamina? Oh, you gods! Look, comrades: the girl
has been captured!

SECOND and THIRD SLAVE
Pamina? What a terrible sight!

111

ERSTER SKLAVE
Seht, wie der unbarmherzige Teufel sie bei ihren zarten Händchen
fasst. Das halt' ich nicht aus!

(geht auf die andere Seite ab)

ZWEITER SKLAVE
Ich noch weniger.

(auch dort ab)

DRITTER SKLAVE
So was sehen zu müssen, ist Höllenmarter!

(ab)

Elfter Auftritt

Monostatos, Pamina, die von Sklaven herein geführt wird

Nr. 6 Terzett

MONOSTATOS *(sehr schnell)*
Du feines Täubchen, nur herein.   [6]

PAMINA
O welche Marter, welche Pein!

MONOSTATOS
Verloren ist dein Leben.

PAMINA
Der Tod macht mich nicht beben;
nur meine Mutter dauert mich,
sie stirbt vor Gram ganz sicherlich.

MONOSTATOS
He Sklaven! legt ihr Fesseln an;
mein Hass soll dich verderben!

(Sie legen ihr Fesseln an.)

FIRST SLAVE
Look how the merciless devil has seized her by her tender hands.
I can't bear it!

(exit on the other side of the stage)

SECOND SLAVE
Nor I!

(exit similarly)

THIRD SLAVE
Having to see this is hell!

(exit)

Scene 11

Monostatos, Pamina, brought in by slaves

No. 6 Trio

MONOSTATOS *(very quickly)*
Come here, my pretty little dove.   [6]

PAMINA
Oh, what torture, what pain!

MONOSTATOS
Your life is over.

PAMINA
I'm not afraid to die,
I'm sad only for my mother:
she will surely die of grief.

MONOSTATOS
Hey, slaves! Put the shackles on her;
my hatred will destroy you.

(They put the shackles on her.)

113

PAMINA
O lass mich lieber sterben,
weil nichts, Barbar, dich rühren kann.

(Sie sinkt ohnmächtig auf ein Sofa.)

MONOSTATOS
Nun fort! Lasst mich bei ihr allein.

(Die Sklaven ab.)

Zwölfter Auftritt

Vorige. Papageno von außen am Fenster, ohne gleich gesehen zu werden.

PAPAGENO
Wo bin ich wohl? Wo mag ich sein?
Aha! da find ich Leute,
gewagt; ich geh herein.

(geht herein)

Schön Mädchen, jung und rein,
viel weißer noch als Kreide ...

(Monostatos und Papageno sehen sich, – erschrecken einer über den andern.)

MONOSTATOS und PAPAGENO
Hu! Das – ist – der – Teu – fel – sich – er – lich!
Hab Mitleid, und verschone mich!
Hu! Hu! Hu!

(Sie laufen beide ab.)

Dreizehnter Auftritt

Pamina allein.

PAMINA *(spricht wie im Traum)*
Mutter – Mutter – Mutter!

(Sie erholt sich, sieht sich um.)

PAMINA
Oh, rather let me die, you monster,
since nothing can move your heart.

(She falls onto a sofa in a faint.)

MONOSTATOS
Off with you! Leave me alone with her.

(The slaves leave.)

Scene 12

The above. Papageno offstage, from the window, without immediately being seen.

PAPAGENO
So where am I? Where might I be?
Aha! There are people there;
I'll be brave and go inside.

(enters)

Pretty girl, young and delicate,
whiter even than chalk…

(Monostatos and Papageno lock eyes, and each takes fright at the other.)

MONOSTATOS and PAPAGENO
Ooh! That – is – the – de – vil – with – out – a – doubt!
Have mercy, and spare me!
Ooh, ooh, ooh!

(They both run off.)

Scene 13

Pamina alone.

PAMINA *(speaking as if in a dream)*
Mother – mother – mother!

(She comes to, and looks round.)

115

Wie? – Noch schlägt dieses Herz? – Noch nicht vernichtet? – Zu neuen Qualen erwacht? – O das ist hart, sehr hart! – Mir bitterer, als der Tod!

Vierzehnter Auftritt

Papageno, Pamina.

PAPAGENO

Bin ich nicht ein Narr, dass ich mich schrecken ließ? Es gibt ja schwarze Vögel in der Welt, warum denn nicht auch schwarze Menschen? – Ah, sieh da! Hier ist das schöne Fräuleinbild noch. – Du Tochter der nächtlichen Königin!

PAMINA

Nächtliche Königin? Wer bist du?

PAPAGENO

Ein Abgesandter der sternflammenden Königin.

PAMINA *(freudig)*

Meiner Mutter? O Wonne! Dein Name?

PAPAGENO

Papageno!

PAMINA

Papageno? Papageno – ich erinnere mich den Namen oft gehört zu haben, dich selbst aber sah ich nie.

PAPAGENO

Ich dich ebensowenig.

PAMINA

Du kennst also meine gute, zärtliche Mutter?

PAPAGENO

Wenn du die Tochter der nächtlichen Königin bist – ja!

PAMINA

O ich bin es.

What? Is my heart still beating? Have I not yet been destroyed? Have I woken to new anguish? Oh, that is hard, very hard! More bitter to me than death.

Scene 14

Papageno, Pamina.

PAPAGENO
How stupid of me to let myself be scared! There are black birds in the world, after all, so why not black people too? Ah, look, the pretty lady's still here. The Queen of the Night's daughter!

PAMINA
Queen of the Night? Who are you?

PAPAGENO
An envoy from the star blazing queen.

PAMINA *(joyfully)*
My mother? Oh, rapture! Your name?

PAPAGENO
Papageno!

PAMINA
Papageno? Papageno – I remember having often heard the name, but I've never seen you myself.

PAPAGENO
Nor have I seen you.

PAMINA
So do you know my kind, tender mother?

PAPAGENO
If you're the daughter of the Queen of the Night – yes!

PAMINA
Yes, I am.

PAPAGENO
Das will ich gleich erkennen.

(Er sieht das Portrait an, welches der Prinz zuvor empfangen, und Papageno nun an einem Bande am Halse trägt.)

Die Augen schwarz – richtig, schwarz. Die Lippen rot – richtig, rot. Blonde Haare – blonde Haare. Alles trifft ein, bis aus Händ' und Füße. Nach dem Gemälde zu schließen, sollst du weder Hände noch Füße haben; denn hier sind auch keine angezeigt.

PAMINA
Erlaube mir – ja ich bin's. Wie kam es in deine Hände?

PAPAGENO
Dir das zu erzählen, wäre zu weitläufig; es kam von Hand zu Hand.

PAMINA
Wie kam es in die deinige?

PAPAGENO
Auf eine wunderbare Art. Ich habe es gefangen.

PAMINA
Gefangen?

PAPAGENO
Ich muss dir umständlicher erzählen. Ich kam heute früh wie gewöhnlich zu deiner Mutter Palast mit meiner Lieferung.

PAMINA
Lieferung?

PAPAGENO
Ja, ich liefere deiner Mutter, und ihren Jungfrauen schon seit vielen Jahren alle die schönen Vögel in den Palast. Eben als ich im Begriff war, meine Vögel abzugeben, sah ich einen Menschen vor mir, der sich Prinz nennen lässt. Dieser Prinz hat deine Mutter so eingenommen, dass sie ihm dein Bildnis schenkte, und ihm befahl, dich zu befreien. Sein Entschluss war so schnell, als seine Liebe zu dir.

PAPAGENO
> I'll just check.

(He looks at the portrait that the Prince received, and which Papageno is now wearing on a ribbon round his neck.)

> Eyes, dark – correct, dark – Lips, red – correct, red – blond hair – blond hair. Everything matches, except for hands and feet. According to this painting, you should have neither hands nor feet, because there aren't any shown here.

PAMINA
> Allow me – yes, that's me. How did this come into your hands?

PAPAGENO
> It would take too long to explain all that. It came to me by hand.

PAMINA
> How did it come into yours?

PAPAGENO
> In an amazing way. I caught it.

PAMINA
> Caught?

PAPAGENO
> I'd better tell you the whole story. Early this morning I came as usual to your mother's palace with my delivery.

PAMINA
> Delivery?

PAPAGENO
> Yes, for several years I've been delivering to the palace all the lovely birds for your mother and her young ladies. Just as I was about to hand over my birds, I saw a man in front of me who called himself Prince. Your mother was so taken with this Prince that she gave him your portrait and commanded him to rescue you. His decision was as rapid as his love for you.

PAMINA
Liebe?

(*freudig*)

Er liebt mich also? O sage mir das noch einmal, ich höre das Wort Liebe gar zu gerne.

PAPAGENO
Das glaube ich dir, ohne zu schwören; bist ja ein Fräuleinbild. – Wo blieb ich denn?

PAMINA
Bei der Liebe.

PAPAGENO
Richtig, bei der Liebe! – Das nenn' ich Gedächtnis haben – kurz also diese große Liebe zu dir war der Peitschenstreich, um unsre Füße in schnellen Gang zu bringen; nun sind wir hier, dir tausend schöne und angenehme Sachen zu sagen; dich in unsre Arme zu nehmen, und, wenn es möglich ist, ebenso schnell, wo nicht schneller als hierher, in den Palast deiner Mutter zu eilen.

PAMINA
Das ist alles sehr schön gesagt; aber lieber Freund! Wenn der unbekannte Jüngling oder Prinz, wie er sich nennt, Liebe für mich fühlt, warum säumt er so lange, mich von meinen Fesseln zu befreien?

PAPAGENO
Da steckt eben der Haken. Wie wir von den Jungfrauen Abschied nahmen, so sagten sie uns, drei holde Knaben würden unsre Wegweiser sein, sie würden uns belehren, wie und auf was Art wir handeln sollen.

PAMINA
Sie lehrten euch?

PAPAGENO
Nichts lehrten sie uns, denn wir haben keinen gesehen. – Zur Sicherheit also war der Prinz so fein, mich voraus zu schicken, um dir unsre Ankunft anzukündigen.

PAMINA
  Love?

(*joyfully*)

  Does he love me, then? Oh, tell me again, I'm so happy to hear
  the word love.

PAPAGENO
  That I can well believe: you are a pretty girl, after all. Where
  was I?

PAMINA
  You'd got to love.

PAPAGENO
  That's right, to love – that's what I call a memory – in a
  word, this great love for you was the spur for us to hurry
  off; now we're here, to tell you countless lovely, pleasant
  things; to take you in our arms and, if possible, just as
  quick, if not quicker than I got here, to hurry off to your
  mother's palace.

PAMINA
  That is all well said; but, my friend, if the unknown young man
  or Prince, as he's called, feels love for me, why does he delay so
  long to free me from my chains?

PAPAGENO
  There's the snag. When we said goodbye to the ladies, they
  told us that three gracious boys would be our guides, that
  they would instruct us on how and in what way we should
  act.

PAMINA
  Did they teach you?

PAPAGENO
  They didn't teach us anything, because we haven't seen them.
  Just to be sure, the Prince was clever enough to send me on
  ahead to tell you about our arrival.

PAMINA

Freund, du hast viel gewagt! Wenn Sarastro dich hier erblicken sollte—

PAPAGENO

So wird mir meine Rückreise erspart – das kann ich mir denken.

PAMINA

Dein martervoller Tod würde ohne Grenzen sein.

PAPAGENO

Um diesem auszuweichen, so gehen wir lieber bei Zeiten.

PAMINA

Wie hoch mag wohl die Sonne sein?

PAPAGENO

Bald gegen Mittag.

PAMINA

So haben wir keine Minute zu versäumen. Um diese Zeit kommt Sarastro gewöhnlich von der Jagd zurück.

PAPAGENO

Sarastro ist also nicht zu Hause? Pah! Da haben wir gewonnenes Spiel! – Komm, schönes Fräuleinbild! Du wirst Augen machen, wenn du den schönen Jüngling erblickst.

PAMINA

Wohl denn, es sei gewagt!

(*Sie gehen, Pamina kehrt um.*)

Aber wenn dies ein Fallstrick wäre – wenn dieser nun ein böser Geist von Sarastros Gefolge wäre?

(*sieht ihn bedenklich an*)

PAPAGENO

Ich ein böser Geist? Wo denkt ihr hin Fräuleinbild? Ich bin der beste Geist von der Welt.

PAMINA

My friend, you've taken a big risk! If Sarastro were to spot you
here—

PAPAGENO

Then I'd be spared my return journey – I can well imagine.

PAMINA

Your agonizing death would know no limits.

PAPAGENO

To avoid that, let's get away quickly.

PAMINA

How high is the sun in the sky?

PAPAGENO

Almost midday.

PAMINA

Then we don't have a moment to spare. Sarastro usually comes
back from hunting at this time.

PAPAGENO

So Sarastro isn't at home? Pah! Then we're home and dry! Come
along, pretty lady – you'll be all eyes when you catch sight of the
handsome young man.

PAMINA

Very well, let's take the risk!

(*They go; Pamina turns round.*)

But what if this were a trap – if this were one of Sarastro's evil
spirits?

(*She looks at him dubiously.*)

PAPAGENO

Me, an evil spirit? What are you thinking of, young lady? I'm the
nicest spirit in the world.

123

PAMINA

Freund, vergib, vergib! Wenn ich dich beleidigte. Du hast ein gefühlvolles Herz, das sehe ich in jedem deiner Züge.

PAPAGENO

Ach freilich hab ich ein gefühlvolles Herz. Aber was nützt mir das alles? Ich möchte mir oft alle meine Federn ausrupfen, wenn ich bedenke, dass Papageno noch keine Papagena hat.

PAMINA

Armer Mann! Du hast also noch kein Weib?

PAPAGENO

Nicht einmal ein Mädchen, viel weniger ein Weib! Ja das ist betrübt! Und unsereiner hat doch auch bisweilen seine lustigen Stunden, wo man gern gesellschaftliche Unterhaltung haben möcht'.

PAMINA

Geduld, Freund! Der Himmel wird auch für dich sorgen; er wird dir eine Freundin schicken, ehe du dir's vermutest.

PAPAGENO

Wenn er's nur bald schickte.

Nr. 7 Duett

PAMINA

Bei Männern, welche Liebe fühlen,   [7]
fehlt auch ein gutes Herze nicht.

PAPAGENO

Die süßen Triebe mitzufühlen,
ist dann der Weiber erste Pflicht.

BEIDE

Wir wollen uns der Liebe freu'n,
wir leben durch die Lieb' allein.

PAMINA

Die Lieb' versüßet jede Plage,
ihr opfert jede Kreatur.

PAMINA

My friend, forgive me if I offended you. You have a sensitive heart – I can tell that from your every feature.

PAPAGENO

Oh yes, I do have a sensitive heart. But what good does that do me? I could rip out all my feathers when I think that Papageno doesn't yet have a Papagena.

PAMINA

You poor man! So you don't have a wife?

PAPAGENO

Not even a girlfriend, let alone a wife. Yes, that's sad! And yet people like us occasionally have times when we enjoy ourselves too, when we'd like some sociable chat.

PAMINA

Be patient, my friend! Heaven will look after you and send you a girlfriend sooner than you expect.

PAPAGENO

If it would only hurry up.

No. 7 Duet

PAMINA

People who can feel love   [7]
have a good heart as well.

PAPAGENO

To feel these sweet instincts
is women's first duty.

BOTH

Let us rejoice in love,
we live for love alone.

PAMINA

Love sweetens all our troubles,
every creature makes sacrifices for it.

PAPAGENO
Sie würzet unsre Lebenstage,
sie wirkt im Kreise der Natur.

BEIDE
Ihr hoher Zweck zeigt deutlich an:
nichts edler sei, als Weib und Mann.
Mann und Weib und Weib und Mann
reichen an die Götter an.

(*beide ab*)

Fünfzehnter Auftritt

Das Theater verwandelt sich in einen Hain. Ganz im Grunde der Bühne ist ein schöner Tempel, worauf diese Worte stehen: „Tempel der Weisheit"; dieser Tempel führt mit Säulen zu zwei andern Tempeln; rechts auf dem einen steht: „Tempel der Vernunft". Links steht: „Tempel der Natur".

Nr. 8 Finale

Drei Knaben führen den Tamino herein, jeder hat einen silbernen Palmzweig in der Hand.   [8a]

DIE DREI KNABEN
Zum Ziele führt dich diese Bahn,
doch musst du, Jüngling, männlich siegen.
Drum höre unsre Lehre an:
sei standhaft, duldsam, und verschwiegen!

TAMINO
Ihr holden Kleinen saget mir an,
ob ich Paminen retten kann.

DIE DREI KNABEN
Dies kund zu tun, steht uns nicht an;
sei standhaft, duldsam, und verschwiegen!
Bedenke dies: kurz, sei ein Mann.
Dann Jüngling wirst du männlich siegen.

(*gehen ab*)

PAPAGENO
> It is the spice of life;
> it works in the circle of nature.

BOTH
> Its higher goal is clear to see,
> there is nothing nobler than man and woman.
> Man and woman, and woman and man,
> reach towards the divine.

(Both leave.)

Scene 15

The scene changes to a grove. At the far back of the stage is a beautiful temple bearing the words 'Temple of Wisdom'; this temple leads via a colonnade to two further temples; on the right-hand one is written 'Temple of Reason', on the left, 'Temple of Nature'.

No. 8 Finale

Three boys lead Tamino on. Each one is holding a silver palm branch. [8a]

THE THREE BOYS
> This path leads you to the goal,
> but, young man, you must manfully triumph.
> So listen to our words:
> be steadfast, patient and prudent!

TAMINO
> Tell me, fair children,
> if I can rescue Pamina.

THE THREE BOYS
> It is not for us to tell you this;
> be steadfast, patient and prudent!
> Remember this, simply be a man.
> Then, young man, you will manfully triumph.

(They leave.)

TAMINO

Die Weisheitslehre dieser Knaben
sei ewig mir ins Herz gegraben.
Wo bin ich nun? Was wird mit mir?
Ist dies der Sitz der Götter hier?
Doch zeigen die Pforten, es zeigen die Säulen,
dass Klugheit und Arbeit und Künste hier weilen.
Wo Tätigkeit thronet, und Müßiggang weicht,
erhält seine Herrschaft das Laster nicht leicht.
Ich wage mich mutig zur Pforte hinein.
Die Absicht ist edel, und lauter und rein.
Erzittre, feiger Bösewicht!
Paminen retten ist mir Pflicht.

(geht an die Pforte rechts, macht sie auf, und als er hinein will, hört man von fern eine Stimme)

EINE STIMME

Zurück!

TAMINO

Zurück? So wag ich hier mein Glück!

(geht an die Pforte links)

EINE STIMME *(von innen)*

Zurück!

TAMINO

Auch hier ruft man zurück?

(sieht sich um)

Da seh' ich noch eine Tür!
Vielleicht find ich den Eingang hier!

(Er klopft, ein alter Priester erscheint.)

PRIESTER

Wo willst du, kühner Fremdling, hin?
Was suchst du hier im Heiligtum?

TAMINO

    Let these boys' words of wisdom
    be engraved for ever on my heart.
    Where am I now? What will become of me?
    Is this where the gods reside?
    The doors and the columns show
    that wisdom, industry and art abide here;
    where diligence rules and idleness retreats,
    vice cannot easily stake its claim.
    Fearlessly I approach the gates,
    my intention is noble, honourable and pure.
    Tremble, cowardly villain!
    To save Pamina is my task.

(goes to the door on the right, opens it and, as he is about to enter, a distant voice is heard)

A VOICE

    Stand back!

TAMINO

    Stand back? Then I'll try my fortune here!

(goes to the door on the left)

A VOICE *(from within)*

    Stand back!

TAMINO

    Here too they shout 'stand back'?

(looks around)

    I see another door there!
    Perhaps I'll find the entrance here.

(He knocks, an elderly priest appears.)

PRIEST

    Bold stranger, where is it you wish to go?
    What are you seeking in the sanctuary?

TAMINO
Der Lieb und Tugend Eigentum.

PRIESTER
Die Worte sind von hohem Sinn –
allein, wie willst du diese finden?
Dich leitet Lieb und Tugend nicht,
weil Tod und Rache dich entzünden.

TAMINO *(schnell)*
Nur Rache für den Bösewicht.

PRIESTER
Den wirst du wohl bei uns nicht finden.

TAMINO
Sarastro herrscht in diesen Gründen?

PRIESTER
Ja, ja! Sarastro herrschet hier!

TAMINO
Doch in dem Weisheitstempel nicht?

PRIESTER *(langsam)*
Er herrscht im Weisheitstempel hier.

TAMINO *(will gehen)*
So ist denn alles Heuchelei!

PRIESTER
Willst du schon wieder gehn?

TAMINO
Ja, ich will gehn, froh und frei –
nie euren Tempel sehn.

PRIESTER
Erklär dich näher mir,
dich täuschet ein Betrug!

TAMINO
The realm of love and virtue.

PRIEST
These words show a lofty mind,
but how do you intend to find them?
You are not led by love and virtue,
for you are spurred by death and vengeance.

TAMINO *(quickly)*
Vengeance only on the villain.

PRIEST
You will not find him here.

TAMINO
Does Sarastro rule here?

PRIEST
Yes, yes, Sarastro rules here.

TAMINO
But not in the Temple of Wisdom?

PRIEST *(slowly)*
He rules here in the Temple of Wisdom.

TAMINO *(makes to go)*
Then all is hypocrisy.

PRIEST
Will you leave so soon?

TAMINO
Yes, I will go, happy and free,
never to see your temple.

PRIEST
Explain yourself more to me,
you have been misled.

131

TAMINO

Sarastro wohnet hier,
das ist mir schon genug!

PRIESTER

Wenn du dein Leben liebst,
so rede, bleibe da!
Sarastro hassest du?

TAMINO

Ich hass' ihn ewig, ja!

PRIESTER

Nun gib mir deine Gründe an!

TAMINO

Er ist ein Unmensch, ein Tyrann!

PRIESTER

Ist das, was du gesagt, erwiesen?

TAMINO

Durch ein unglücklich Weib bewiesen,
die Gram und Jammer niederdrückt!

PRIESTER

Ein Weib hat also dich berückt?
Ein Weib tut wenig, plaudert viel.
Du Jüngling glaubst dem Zungenspiel?
O legte doch Sarastro dir
die Absicht seiner Handlung für—

TAMINO

Die Absicht ist nur allzu klar!
Riss nicht der Räuber ohn' Erbarmen
Paminen aus der Mutter Armen?

PRIESTER

Ja, Jüngling, was du sagst, ist wahr!

TAMINO

Sarastro dwells here –
that is enough for me.

PRIEST

If you love your life,
then speak – wait!
Do you hate Sarastro?

TAMINO

There is no limit to my hatred of him, yes!

PRIEST

Now tell me your reasons.

TAMINO

He is a monster, a tyrant!

PRIEST

Is there proof for what you say?

TAMINO

The proof of an unhappy woman
oppressed by grief and sorrow.

PRIEST

So has a woman beguiled you?
Women do little and chatter a lot.
Young man, do you believe their wagging tongues?
Oh, if Sarastro were to reveal to you
the purpose of his action—

TAMINO

The purpose is all too clear!
Did he not mercilessly snatch
Pamina from her mother's arms?

PRIEST

Yes, young man, what you say is true.

TAMINO
　Wo ist sie, die er uns geraubt?
　Man opferte vielleicht sie schon?

PRIESTER
　Dir dies zu sagen, teurer Sohn,
　ist jetzund mir noch nicht erlaubt.

TAMINO
　Erklär dies Rätsel, täusch mich nicht!

PRIESTER
　Die Zunge bindet Eid und Pflicht!

TAMINO
　Wann also wird die Decke schwinden?

PRIESTER
　Sobald dich führt der Freundschaft Hand
　ins Heiligtum zum ew'gen Band.

(geht ab)

TAMINO *(allein)*
　O ew'ge Nacht! Wann wirst du schwinden?
　Wann wird das Licht mein Auge finden?

CHOR *(von innen)*
　Bald Jüngling, oder nie!

TAMINO
　Bald sagt ihr, oder nie?　　　　　　　　　　[8b]
　Ihr Unsichtbaren, saget mir:
　lebt denn Pamina noch?

CHOR *(von innen)*
　Pamina lebet noch!

TAMINO *(freudig)*
　Sie lebt? Ich danke euch dafür.

(nimmt seine Flöte heraus)

TAMINO
Where is she, who was robbed from us?
Has she perhaps been sacrificed already?

PRIEST
My dear son, I am not yet permitted
to tell you this.

TAMINO
Explain this puzzle – don't trick me.

PRIEST
My vow and duty bind my tongue.

TAMINO
Then when will the mystery become clear?

PRIEST
As soon as the hand of friendship
leads you to the sanctuary's eternal Brotherhood.

(exit)

TAMINO *(alone)*
O endless night! When will you fade away?
When shall I see the light?

CHORUS *(from within)*
Soon, young man, or never!

TAMINO
Soon, you say, or never?   [8b]
Unseen ones, tell me,
is Pamina still alive?

CHORUS *(from within)*
Pamina is still alive!

TAMINO *(joyfully)*
She's alive? For that I thank you.

(He takes out his flute.)

135

O wenn ich doch nur im Stande wäre,
Allmächtige, zu Eurer Ehre,
mit jedem Tone meinen Dank,
zu schildern, wie er hier *(aufs Herz deutend)* entsprang!

(Er spielt, sogleich kommen Tiere von allen Arten hervor, ihm zuzuhören. Er hört auf, und sie fliehen. Die Vögel pfeifen dazu.) [8c]

Wie stark ist nicht dein Zauberton,
weil, holde Flöte, durch dein Spielen
selbst wilde Tiere Freude fühlen.
Doch nur Pamina bleibt davon.

(spielt)

Pamina!

(spielt)

Höre mich!

(spielt)

Umsonst!

(spielt)

Wo?

(spielt)

Ach, wo find ich dich?

(Er spielt, Papageno antwortet von innen mit seinem Flötchen.)

Ha, das ist Papagenos Ton!

(Er spielt, Papageno antwortet.)

Vielleicht sah er Paminen schon!
Vielleicht eilt sie mit ihm zu mir!
Vielleicht führt mich der Ton zu ihr.

(eilt ab)

Almighty beings, if I were only able
to demonstrate my thanks
with every note, to your honour,
as it sprang from here *(pointing to his heart)* within!

(As soon as he plays, animals of every kind emerge to listen to him. He stops, and they run away. The birds sing along with his playing.)   [8c]

What power there is in your magic sound
if even wild animals feel joy
to hear you play, charming flute.
Only Pamina does not come;

(plays)

Pamina!

(plays)

Hear me!

(plays)

In vain!

(plays)

Where?

(plays)

Ah, where can I find you?

(He plays, and Papageno replies with his pipes from offstage.)

Ha, that is Papageno's sound.

(He plays, Papageno replies.)

Perhaps he's already seen Pamina,
perhaps he's hurrying with her to me!
Perhaps the sound will lead me to her.

(hurries off)

Sechzehnter Auftritt

Papageno, Pamina ohne Fesseln.

BEIDE
Schnelle Füße, rascher Mut,
schützt vor Feindes List und Wut.
Fänden wir Taminen doch!
Sonst erwischen sie uns noch!

PAMINA
Holder Jüngling!

PAPAGENO
Stille, stille, ich kann's besser!

(*Er pfeift. Tamino antwortet von innen mit seiner Flöte.*)

BEIDE
Welche Freude ist wohl größer,
Freund Tamino hört uns schon,
hieher kam der Flötenton.
Welch' ein Glück, wenn ich ihn finde.
Nur geschwinde! Nur geschwinde!

(*wollen hineingehen*)

Siebzehnter Auftritt

Vorige, Monostatos.

MONOSTATOS (*ihrer spottend*)
Nur geschwinde, nur geschwinde…
Ha! Hab ich euch noch erwischt!
Nur herbei mit Stahl und Eisen;
wart, man wird euch Mores weisen!
Den Monostatos berücken!
Nur herbei mit Band und Stricken;
he, ihr Sklaven kommt herbei!

(*Die Sklaven kommen mit Fesseln.*)

Scene 16

Papageno, Pamina, freed of her shackles.

BOTH
Swift feet, speedy courage
protect us from the enemy's cunning and rage.
But if only we could find Tamino!
Otherwise they'll catch us again.

PAMINA
Dear young man!

PAPAGENO
Quiet, quiet! I can do it better!

(He plays. Tamino, offstage, replies with his flute.)

BOTH
What joy could be greater,
our friend Tamino hears us;
the sound of the flute travelled here.
What happiness if I find him.
Only hurry! Only hurry!

(making to go)

Scene 17

The above, Monostatos.

MONOSTATOS *(mocking them)*
Only hurry! Only hurry...
Ha, now I've caught you again!
Now come here with steel and iron;
just wait – you're going to learn
not to fool Monostatos!
Come here with ropes and ties;
hey, slaves, come here!

(The slaves come with shackles.)

PAMINA und PAPAGENO
  Ach! Nun ist's mit uns vorbei!

PAPAGENO
  Wer viel wagt, gewinnt oft viel!
  Komm du schönes Glockenspiel,
  lass die Glöckchen klingen, klingen,
  dass die Ohren ihnen singen.

(schlägt auf sein Instrument)

MONOSTATOS und SKLAVEN
  Das klinget so herrlich, das klinget so schön!
  Larala, larala!
  Nie hab ich so etwas gehört und gesehn!
  Larala, larala!

(gehen marschmäßig ab)

PAMINA und PAPAGENO (lachen)
  Könnte jeder brave Mann
  solche Glöckchen finden,
  seine Feinde würden dann
  ohne Mühe schwinden.
  Und er lebte ohne sie
  in der besten Harmonie!
  Nur der Freundschaft Harmonie
  mildert die Beschwerden,
  ohne diese Sympathie
  ist kein Glück auf Erden.

CHOR (von innen)
  Es lebe Sarastro, Sarastro lebe!

PAPAGENO
  Was soll dies bedeuten? Ich zittre, ich bebe!

PAMINA
  O Freund! Nun ist's um uns getan!
  Dies kündigt den Sarastro an!

PAMINA and PAPAGENO
Now we're done for.

PAPAGENO
Fortune often favours the bold.
Come, you lovely glockenspiel!
Let the little bells ring and ring
to make their ears hum.

(plays his instrument.)

MONOSTATOS and SLAVES
That sounds so wonderful, that sounds so lovely!
Larala, larala!
I've never heard or seen the like!
Larala, larala!

(go marching off)

PAMINA and PAPAGENO *(laughing)*
If every honest man
could find bells such as these,
his foes would then
effortlessly disappear.
And without them he would live
in the greatest harmony!
Only the harmony of friendship
soothes our troubles;
without this accord
there is no happiness on earth.

CHORUS *(from within)*
Long live Sarastro! May Sarastro live long!

PAPAGENO
What can that mean? I'm frightened, I'm shaking.

PAMINA
My friend, now we're in trouble!
That heralds Sarastro's approach.

PAPAGENO

O wär ich eine Maus,
wie wollt ich mich verstecken –
wär ich so klein wie Schnecken,
so kröch ich in mein Haus!
Mein Kind, was werden wir nun sprechen?

PAMINA

Die Wahrheit – die Wahrheit!
Sei sie auch Verbrechen!

Achtzehnter Auftritt

Vorige, ein Zug von Gefolge; zuletzt fährt Sarastro auf einem Triumphwagen heraus, der von sechs Löwen gezogen wird.

CHOR

Es lebe Sarastro, Sarastro soll leben!
Er ist es, dem wir uns mit Freuden ergeben!
Stets mög er des Lebens als Weiser sich freun. –
Er ist unser Abgott, dem alle sich weihn.

(Dieser Chor wird gesungen, bis Sarastro aus dem Wagen ist.)

PAMINA *(kniet)*

Herr, ich bin zwar Verbrecherin!
Ich wollte deiner Macht entfliehn.
Allein die Schuld ist nicht an mir!
Der böse Mohr verlangte Liebe,
darum, o Herr, entfloh ich dir!

SARASTRO

Steh auf, erheitre dich, o Liebe;
denn ohne erst in dich zu dringen,
weiß ich von deinem Herzen mehr,
Du liebest einen andern sehr.
Zur Liebe will ich dich nicht zwingen,
doch geb' ich dir die Freiheit nicht.

PAPAGENO

> I wish I were a mouse!
> How I'd like to hide;
> if I were as small as a snail
> I'd crawl into my house.
> My child, what shall we say now?

PAMINA

> The truth, the truth!
> Even though it be a crime!

Scene 18

The above, a procession of attendants; Sarastro drives on last in a triumphal carriage drawn by six lions.

CHORUS

> Long live Sarastro, long may Sarastro live!
> It is to him that we joyfully devote ourselves!
> May he ever enjoy life in wisdom!
> He is our master, whom we worship.

(This chorus is sung until Sarastro has stepped down from the carriage.)

PAMINA *(kneels)*

> Sir, I have indeed done wrong!
> I wanted to escape your power.
> But I am not to blame –
> the evil Moor demanded love;
> that's why I ran away from you, sir.

SARASTRO

> Rise, be cheered, O dear one;
> for without even questioning you
> I know more what is in your heart:
> you love another deeply.
> I shall not force you to love,
> but neither shall I set you free.

143

PAMINA

Mich rufet ja die Kindespflicht,
denn meine Mutter—

SARASTRO

steht in meiner Macht.
Du würdest um dein Glück gebracht,
wenn ich dich ihren Händen ließe.

PAMINA

Mir klingt der Mutter Name süße;
sie ist es—

SARASTRO

und ein stolzes Weib.
Ein Mann muss eure Herzen leiten,
denn ohne ihn pflegt jedes Weib
aus ihrem Wirkungskreis zu schreiten.

Neunzehnter Auftritt

Vorige, Monostatos, Tamino

MONOSTATOS

Na, stolzer Jüngling; nur hierher!
Hier ist Sarastro, unser Herr!

PAMINA und TAMINO

Er/sie ist's!

PAMINA

Ich glaub es kaum!

PAMINA und TAMINO

Er/sie ist's!

TAMINO

Es ist kein Traum!

PAMINA und TAMINO

Es schling' mein Arm sich um ihn/sie her,
und wenn es auch mein Ende wär'!

PAMINA
I have a duty as a child,
for my mother—

SARASTRO
is within my power.
All your happiness would vanish
if I delivered you into her hands.

PAMINA
The name of mother sounds sweet to me;
that is who she is—

SARASTRO
and a proud woman.
A man must guide your hearts,
for without one, a woman
cannot fulfil her destiny.

Scene 19

The above, Monostatos, Tamino

MONOSTATOS
Now come here, proud young man!
Here is Sarastro, our lord!

PAMINA and TAMINO
It is he/she!

PAMINA
I can scarcely believe it!

PAMINA and TAMINO
It is he/she!

TAMINO
This is no dream!

PAMINA and TAMINO
I embrace him/her,
even if it means the end for me!

145

CHOR

Was soll das heißen?

MONOSTATOS

Welch eine Dreistigkeit!
Gleich auseinander, das geht zu weit!

(trennt sie, kniet)

Dein Sklave liegt zu deinen Füßen,
lass den verweg'nen Frevler büßen.
Bedenk, wie frech der Knabe ist!
Durch dieses seltnen Vogels List
wollt er Paminen dir entführen,
allein, ich wusst ihn auszuspüren.
Du kennst mich! Meine Wachsamkeit—

SARASTRO

Verdient, dass man ihr Lorbeer streut!
He! Gebt dem Ehrenmann sogleich—

MONOSTATOS

Schon deine Gnade macht mich reich!

SARASTRO

Nur siebenundsiebzig Sohlenstreich.

MONOSTATOS

Ach, Herr, den Lohn verhofft ich nicht.

SARASTRO

Nicht Dank! Es ist ja meine Pflicht!

(Monostatos wird fortgeführt.)

CHOR

Es lebe Sarastro, der göttliche Weise,
er lohnet und strafet in ähnlichem Kreise.

SARASTRO

Führt diese beiden Fremdlinge
in unsern Prüfungstempel ein,

146

CHORUS
What is going on?

MONOSTATOS
Such insolence!
Get away from each other at once – this is going too far!

(separates them, then kneels)

Your slave lies at your feet;
let the rash evildoer be punished.
Consider how brazen the boy is!
Through the cunning of this strange bird,
he tried to abduct Pamina;
but I found him out.
You know me! My vigilance—

SARASTRO
You will receive your just reward!
Ho! Give this gentleman at once—

MONOSTATOS
Your favour is reward enough.

SARASTRO
No more than seventy-seven strokes on his soles!

MONOSTATOS
Ah, sir! That is not the reward I hoped for.

SARASTRO
Do not thank me! It is only my duty.

(Monostatos is led off.)

CHORUS
Long live Sarastro, divinely wise;
he rewards and punishes alike.

SARASTRO
Lead these two strangers
into our Temple of Trials:

bedecket ihre Häupter dann –
sie müssen erst gereinigt sein.

(Zwei Priester bringen eine Art Sack und bedecken die Häupter der beiden Fremden.)

CHOR
Wenn Tugend und Gerechtigkeit
den großen Pfad mit Ruhm bestreut,
dann ist die Erd' ein Himmelreich,
und Sterbliche den Göttern gleich.

then cover their heads –
for first they must be purified.

(Two priests bring a kind of sack and cover the heads of the two strangers.)

CHORUS
When virtue and justice
mark the great path with glory,
then earth is a kingdom of heaven,
and mortals become like gods.

ZWEITER AKT

Erster Auftritt

Das Theater ist ein Palmwald; alle Bäume sind silberartig, die Blätter von Gold. Achtzehn Sitze von Blättern; auf einem jeden Sitze steht eine Pyramide, und ein großes schwarzes Horn mit Gold gefasst. In der Mitte ist die größte Pyramide, auch die größten Bäume.

Sarastro nebst andern Priestern kommen in feierlichen Schritten, jeder mit einem Palmzweige in der Hand.

Nr. 9 Marsch der Priester [9]

SARASTRO *(nach einer Pause)*
Ihr, in dem Weisheitstempel eingeweihten Diener der großen Götter Osiris und Isis! Mit reiner Seele erklär ich euch, dass unsre heutige Versammlung eine der wichtigsten unserer Zeit ist. Tamino, ein Königssohn, zwanzig Jahre seines Alters, wandelt an der nördlichen Pforte unsers Tempels, und seufzt mit tugendvollem Herzen nach einem Gegenstande, den wir alle Mühe und Fließ erringen müssen. Kurz, dieser Jüngling will seinen nächtlichen Schleier von sich reißen, und ins Heiligtum des größten Lichtes blicken. Diesen Tugendhaften zu bewachen, ihm freundschaftlich die Hand zu bieten, sei heute eine unsrer wichtigsten Pflichten.

ERSTER PRIESTER *(steht auf)*
Er besitzt Tugend?

SARASTRO
Tugend!

ACT TWO

Scene 1

The scene is a palm grove, where all the trees are silvery and the leaves are gold. Eighteen seats made of leaves; on each one is a pyramid and great black horn cast in gold. In the middle is the largest pyramid, and the tallest trees as well.

Sarastro enters together with other priests in a celebratory procession, each one carrying a palm branch.

No. 9 March of the Priests [9]

SARASTRO *(after a pause)*
You, initiated servants in the Temple of Wisdom of the great gods Osiris and Isis! With a pure soul I declare to you that our gathering today is one of the most important of our time. Tamino, the son of a king, aged twenty, is journeying to our Temple's north gates, and with virtue in his heart yearns for something that we all must labour to achieve. In a word, this young man wishes to tear away the veils of darkness and look in to the sanctuary of the greatest light. Let one of your most important duties today be to watch over this virtuous man and extend the hand of friendship to him.

FIRST PRIEST *(stands)*
Does he possess virtue?

SARASTRO
Virtue!

151

ZWEITER PRIESTER
Auch Verschwiegenheit?

SARASTRO
Verschwiegenheit!

DRITTER PRIESTER
Ist wohltätig?

SARASTRO
Wohltätig! Haltet ihr ihn für würdig, so folgt meinem Beispiel.

(Sie blasen dreimal in die Hörner.)

Gerührt über die Einigkeit eurer Herzen, dankt Sarastro euch im Namen der Menschheit. Mag immer das Vorurteil seinen Tadel über uns Eingeweihte auslassen! Weisheit und Vernunft zerstückt es gleich dem Spinnengewebe. Unsere Säulen erschüttern sie nie. Jedoch das böse Vorurteil soll schwinden; und es wird schwinden, sobald Tamino selbst die Größe unserer schweren Kunst besitzen wird. Pamina, das sanfte, tugendhafte Mädchen, haben die Götter dem holden Jünglinge bestimmt; dies ist der Grundstein, warum ich sie der stolzen Mutter entriss. Das Weib dünkt sich groß zu sein; hofft durch Blendwerk und Aberglauben das Volk zu berücken, und unsern festen Tempelbau zu zerstören. Allein, das soll sie nicht. Tamino, der holde Jüngling selbst, soll ihn mit uns befestigen und als Eingeweihter der Tugend Lohn, dem Laster aber Strafe sein.

(Der dreimalige Akkord in den Hörnern wird von allen wiederholt.)

SPRECHER *(steht auf)*
Großer Sarastro, deine weisheitsvollen Reden erkennen und bewundern wir; allein, wird Tamino auch die harten Prüfungen, so seiner warten, bekämpfen? Verzeih, dass ich so frei bin, dir meinen Zweifel zu eröffnen! Mich bangt es um den Jüngling. Wenn nun im Schmerz dahingesunken sein Geist ihn verließe, und er dem harten Kampfe unterläge? Er ist Prinz!

SARASTRO
Noch mehr – er ist Mensch!

SECOND PRIEST
And discretion?

SARASTRO
Discretion!

THIRD PRIEST
Is he charitable?

SARASTRO
Charitable! If you consider him worthy, then follow my example.

(They blow the horns three times.)

Moved by your heartfelt accord, Sarastro thanks you in the name of humanity. Even though wicked prejudice may hurl its reproaches at us Initiates, wisdom and reason destroy it like a spider's web. Our columns stand firm against it. Wicked prejudice shall disappear, and it will, as soon as Tamino himself possesses our craft in all its magnitude. The gods have chosen the gentle, virtuous maiden Pamina for the fair young man; this is the reason why I took her away from her proud mother. That woman believes in her own greatness, she hopes through deception and superstition to beguile the people and destroy our solid temple building. But she shall not. Tamino, the worthy youth himself, will fortify it with us and, initiated in reward for his virtue, will punish evil.

(They repeat the three chords on the horns.)

SPEAKER *(stands)*
Great Sarastro, we acknowledge and marvel at your wise words; but will Tamino withstand the taxing trials that await him? Forgive me for revealing my doubts to you so freely. I fear for the young man. What if his spirit, sunk in distress, deserts him, and he succumbs under the hard struggles? He is a Prince!

SARASTRO
More than that – he is a man!

153

SPRECHER
Wenn er nun aber in seiner frühen Jugend leblos erblasste?

SARASTRO
Dann ist er Osiris und Isis gegeben, und wird der Götter Freuden
früher fühlen als wir.

(Der dreimalige Akkord wird wiederholt.)

Man führe Tamino mit seinem Reisegefährten in den Vorhof des
Tempels ein.

(zum Sprecher, der vor ihm niederkniet)

Und du, Freund, den die Götter durch uns zum Verteidiger der
Wahrheit bestimmten – vollziehe dein heiliges Amt, und lehre
durch deine Weisheit beide, was Pflicht der Menschheit sei, lehre
sie die Macht der Götter erkennen.

*(Sprecher geht mit einem Priester ab, alle Priester stellen sich mit
ihren Palmzweigen zusammen.)*

Nr. 10 Arie mit Chor

SARASTRO
O Isis und Osiris, schenket   [10]
der Weisheit Geist dem neuen Paar!
Die ihr der Wandrer Schritte lenket,
stärkt mit Geduld sie in Gefahr.

CHOR
Stärkt mit Geduld sie in Gefahr.

SARASTRO
Lasst sie der Prüfung Früchte sehen.
Doch sollten sie zu Grabe gehen,
so lohnt der Tugend kühnen Lauf,
nehmt sie in euren Wohnsitz auf!

CHOR
Nehmt sie in euren Wohnsitz auf!

(Sarastro geht voraus, dann alle ihm nach ab.)

SPEAKER
What if he were to perish while still young?

SARASTRO
Then he will be given to Osiris and Isis, and will experience the joys of the gods before us.

(The three chords are repeated.)

Lead Tamino and his companion into the forecourt of the Temple.

(to the Speaker, who is kneeling before him)

And you, friend, whom, through us, the gods have chosen as the defender of truth, carry out your sacred task, and teach both men through wisdom what the duty of mankind is, teach them to acknowledge the might of the gods.

(The Speaker goes out with one priest; all the other priests gather together with their palm branches.)

No. 10 Aria with chorus

SARASTRO
O Isis and Osiris, send   [10]
the spirit of wisdom to the two newcomers.
You who guide the wanderer's steps,
strengthen them with patience in danger.

CHORUS
Strengthen them with patience in danger.

SARASTRO
Let them see the fruits of their trials.
but if they should go to the grave,
grant the reward for their courage and virtue,
receive them into your abode!

CHORUS
Receive them into your abode!

(Sarastro leaves first, and the others follow.)

155

Zweiter Auftritt

Nacht, der Donner rollt von weitem. Das Theater verwandelt sich in einen kurzen Vorhof des Tempels, wo man Ruinen von eingefallenen Säulen und Pyramiden sieht, nebst einigen Dornbüschen. An beiden Seiten stehen praktikable hohe altägyptische Türen, welche mehr Seitengebäude vorstellen.

Tamino und Papageno werden vom Sprecher und dem andern Priester hereingeführt; sie lösen ihnen die Säcke ab; die Priester gehen dann ab.

TAMINO
Eine schreckliche Nacht! – Papageno, bist du noch bei mir?

PAPAGENO
I' freilich!

TAMINO
Wo denkst du, dass wir uns nun befinden?

PAPAGENO
Wo? Ja wenn's nicht finster wäre, wollt' ich dir's schon sagen – aber so—

(Donnerschlag)

O weh!—

TAMINO
Was ist's?

PAPAGENO
Mir wird nicht wohl bei der Sache!

TAMINO
Du hast Furcht, wie ich höre.

PAPAGENO
Furcht eben nicht, nur eiskalt läuft's mir über den Rücken.

(starker Donnerschlag)

O weh!

Scene 2

Night, distant thunder. The scene changes to a small temple forecourt, where the ruins of collapsed columns and pyramids can be seen, as well as some thorn bushes. On both sides are tall, practicable ancient Egyptian doors that suggest further buildings to the side.

Tamino and Papageno are led in by the Speaker and another priest; they remove the sacks from their heads; the priests then leave.

TAMINO
A dreadful night! Papageno, are you still with me?

PAPAGENO
Well, yes!

TAMINO
Where do you think we are now?

PAPAGENO
Where? Well, if it weren't so dark I'd be able to tell you – but like this—

(thunder)

Oh no!—

TAMINO
What is it?

PAPAGENO
I'm not having a good feeling about this!

TAMINO
I can hear that you're afraid.

PAPAGENO
Not afraid, just an ice-cold shiver down my spine.

(loud thunderclap)

Oh, no!

TAMINO
Was soll's?

PAPAGENO
Ich glaube, ich bekomme ein kleines Fieber.

TAMINO
Pfui, Papageno! Sei ein Mann!

PAPAGENO
Ich wollt', ich wär' ein Mädchen!

(*ein sehr starker Donnerschlag*)

O! O! O! Das ist mein letzter Augenblick.

Dritter Auftritt

Vorige. Sprecher und der andere Priester mit Fackeln.

SPRECHER
Ihr Fremdlinge, was sucht oder fordert ihr von uns? Was treibt euch an, in unsre Mauern zu dringen?

TAMINO
Freundschaft und Liebe.

SPRECHER
Bist du bereit, es mit deinem Leben zu erkämpfen?

TAMINO
Ja!

SPRECHER
Auch wenn Tod dein Los wäre?

TAMINO
Ja!

SPRECHER
Prinz! Noch ist's Zeit zu weichen – einen Schritt weiter, und es ist zu spät.

TAMINO
  What's wrong?

PAPAGENO
  I think I'm coming down with a bit of a fever.

TAMINO
  For goodness' sake, Papageno! Be a man!

PAPAGENO
  I'd rather be a girl!

(very loud thunderclap)

  Oh! Oh! Oh! My last moment has come.

Scene 3

The above, the Speaker and another priest with torches.

SPEAKER
  Strangers, what are you seeking or demanding from us? What
  has led you to enter within our walls?

TAMINO
  Friendship and love.

SPEAKER
  Are you ready to fight for them with your life?

TAMINO
  Yes!

SPEAKER
  Even if it meant your death?

TAMINO
  Yes!

SPEAKER
  Prince, there is still time to turn back – one step more, and it will
  be too late.

TAMINO
Weisheitslehre sei mein Sieg; Pamina, das holde Mädchen mein Lohn.

SPRECHER
Du unterziehst jeder Prüfung dich?

TAMINO
Jeder!

SPRECHER
Reiche deine Hand mir!

(*Sie reichen sich die Hände.*)

So!

ZWEITER PRIESTER
Ehe du weitersprichst, erlaube mir ein paar Worte mit diesem Fremdlinge zu sprechen. Willst auch du dir Weisheitsliebe erkämpfen?

PAPAGENO
Kämpfen ist meine Sache nicht. Ich verlang' auch im Grunde gar keine Weisheit. Ich bin so ein Naturmensch, der sich mit Schlaf, Speise und Trank begnügt – und wenn es ja sein könnte, dass ich mir einmal ein schönes Weibchen fange.

ZWEITER PRIESTER
Die wirst du nie erhalten, wenn du dich nicht unsern Prüfungen unterziehst.

PAPAGENO
Worin besteht diese Prüfung?

ZWEITER PRIESTER
Dich allen unsern Gesetzen unterwerfen, selbst den Tod nicht scheuen.

PAPAGENO
Ich bleibe ledig!

SPRECHER
Aber wenn du dir ein tugendhaftes, schönes Mädchen erwerben könntest?

TAMINO
Let my victory be the teachings of wisdom; Pamina, the fair maiden, my reward.

SPEAKER
Will you submit to every trial?

TAMINO
Every one!

SPEAKER
Give me your hand!

(They clasp hands.)

So!

SECOND PRIEST
Before you speak again, let me say a few words to this stranger. Do you also wish to strive for the love of wisdom?

PAPAGENO
Striving isn't really my thing. I don't actually want any wisdom. I'm a simple fellow, content with sleeping, eating and drinking, if I could just find myself a pretty wife.

SECOND PRIEST
You will never attain her if you do not undergo our trials.

PAPAGENO
What do these trials consist of?

SECOND PRIEST
Submitting to all our laws, not shrinking even from death.

PAPAGENO
I'll stay single!

SPEAKER
But what if you could win a virtuous, pretty girl for yourself?

161

PAPAGENO
Ich bleibe ledig!

ZWEITER PRIESTER
Wenn nun aber Sarastro dir ein Mädchen aufbewahrt hätte, das
an Farbe und Kleidung dir ganz gleich wäre?

PAPAGENO
Mir gleich! Ist sie jung?

ZWEITER PRIESTER
Jung und schön!

PAPAGENO
Und heißt?

ZWEITER PRIESTER
Papagena.

PAPAGENO
Wie? Pa?

ZWEITER PRIESTER
Papagena!

PAPAGENO
Papagena? Die möcht' ich aus bloßer Neugierde sehen.

ZWEITER PRIESTER
Sehen kannst du sie!

PAPAGENO
Aber wenn ich sie gesehen habe, hernach muss ich sterben?

(*Zweiter Priester macht eine zweideutige Pantomime.*)

PAPAGENO
Ja? Ich bleibe ledig!

ZWEITER PRIESTER
Sehen kannst du sie, aber bis zur verlaufenen Zeit kein Wort mit
ihr sprechen; wird dein Geist so viel Standhaftigkeit besitzen,
deine Zunge in Schranken zu halten?

PAPAGENO
I'll stay single!

SECOND PRIEST
But what if Sarastro had a girl in store for you who was just like you, in colour and clothing?

PAPAGENO
Just like me! Is she young?

SECOND PRIEST
Young and beautiful!

PAPAGENO
And her name?

SECOND PRIEST
Papagena.

PAPAGENO
What? Pa?

SECOND PRIEST
Papagena!

PAPAGENO
Papagena? I'd like to see her, just out of curiosity.

SECOND PRIEST
You can see her!

PAPAGENO
But when I've seen her, will I have to die afterwards?

(The Second Priest's gestures are ambiguous.)

PAPAGENO
Yes? I'll stay single!

SECOND PRIEST
You can see her, but not say a word to her until the allotted time – will your spirit be steadfast enough for you to hold your tongue?

PAPAGENO
O ja!

ZWEITER PRIESTER
Deine Hand! Du sollst sie sehen.

SPRECHER
Auch dir, Prinz, legen die Götter ein heilsames Stillschweigen auf;
ohne dieses seid ihr beide verloren. Du wirst Pamina sehen – aber
nie sie sprechen dürfen; dies ist der Anfang eurer Prüfungszeit.

Nr. 11 Duett

ZWEITE PRIESTER und SPRECHER
Bewahret euch vor Weibertücken, [11]
dies ist des Bundes erste Pflicht;
manch weiser Mann ließ sich berücken,
er fehlte, und versah sich's nicht.
Verlassen sah er sich am Ende,
vergolten seine Treu mit Hohn!
Vergebens rang er seine Hände,
Tod und Verzweiflung war sein Lohn.

(beide Priester ab)

Vierter Auftritt

Tamino, Papageno

PAPAGENO
He, Lichter her! Lichter her! Das ist doch wunderlich, so oft einen
die Herrn verlassen, so sieht man mit offenen Augen nichts.

TAMINO
Ertrag es mit Geduld, und denke, es ist Götter Wille.

Fünfter Auftritt

Vorige, die drei Damen aus der Versenkung

Nr. 12 Quintett

PAPAGENO
    Oh yes!

SECOND PRIEST
    Your hand! You may see her.

SPEAKER
    The gods impose a salutary silence on you too, Prince; otherwise
    you are both lost. You will see Pamina, but are not allowed to
    speak to her at all; your time of trial has begun.

No. 11 Duet

SECOND PRIEST and SPEAKER
    The first duty of the Brotherhood   [11]
    is to beware the wiles of women!
    Many wise men have let themselves be taken in;
    they have erred and been misled.
    They have found themselves abandoned,
    their trust repaid with mockery!
    They wrung their hands in vain,
    death and despair were their reward.

(Both priests leave.)

Scene 4

Tamino, Papageno

PAPAGENO
    Hey, lights over here! Lights over here! That's amazing, every time
    the fellows leave you, you can't see anything with your eyes open.

TAMINO
    Bear it with patience and consider it the will of the gods.

Scene 5

The above, the Three Ladies emerging from the trapdoor.

No. 12 Quintet

DIE DREI DAMEN

Wie? Wie? Wie? [12]
Ihr an diesem Schreckensort?
Nie! Nie! Nie!
Kommt ihr wieder glücklich fort!
Tamino, dir ist Tod geschworen!
Du, Papageno, bist verloren!

PAPAGENO

Nein, nein, nein, das wär zu viel.

TAMINO

Papageno, schweige still!
Willst du dein Gelübde brechen,
nichts mit Weibern hier zu sprechen?

PAPAGENO

Du hörst ja, wir sind beide hin!

TAMINO

Stille, sag ich – schweige still!

PAPAGENO

Immer still und immer still!

DIE DREI DAMEN

Ganz nah ist euch die Königin,
sie drang in Tempel heimlich ein!

PAPAGENO

Wie? Was? Sie soll im Tempel sein?

TAMINO

Stille, sag ich! – schweige still!
Wirst du immer so vermessen
deiner Eidespflicht vergessen?

DIE DREI DAMEN

Tamino, hör! Du bist verloren!
Gedenke an die Königin!
Man zischelt viel sich in die Ohren
von dieser Priester falschem Sinn!

THE THREE LADIES
    What? What? What?   [12]
    You in this fearful place?
    Never, never, never
    will you be fortunate enough to escape!
    Tamino, you're doomed to die!
    You, Papageno, are lost!

PAPAGENO
    No, no, no, that would be too much.

TAMINO
    Papageno, keep silent!
    Do you mean to break your vow
    not to speak with women here?

PAPAGENO
    You heard: we're both doomed.

TAMINO
    Silence, I say! Keep silent!

PAPAGENO
    Always silent, and silent again!

THE THREE LADIES
    The Queen is very close to you!
    She has secretly got inside the temple.

PAPAGENO
    How? What? She's in the temple?

TAMINO
    Silence, I say! Keep silent!
    Are you always going foolishly to
    forget your dutiful vow ?

THE THREE LADIES
    Tamino, listen, you are lost!
    Think of the Queen!
    Whispers abound
    about the falseness of these priests.

167

TAMINO *(für sich)*
Ein Weiser prüft und achtet nicht,
was der gemeine Pöbel spricht.

DIE DREI DAMEN
Man sagt, wer ihrem Bunde schwört,
der fährt zur Höll mit Haut und Haar.

PAPAGENO
Das wär der Teufel! Unerhört!
Sagt an, Tamino, ist das wahr?

TAMINO
Geschwätz, von Weibern nachgesagt,
von Heuchlern aber ausgedacht.

PAPAGENO
Doch sagt es auch die Königin!

TAMINO
Sie ist ein Weib, hat Weibersinn!
Sei still, mein Wort sei dir genug,
denk deiner Pflicht, und handle klug.

DIE DREI DAMEN *(zu Tamino)*
Warum bist du mit uns so spröde?

(Tamino deutet bescheiden, dass er nicht sprechen darf.)

Auch Papageno schweigt. – So rede!

PAPAGENO *(zu den Damen, heimlich)*
Ich möchte gerne – woll—

TAMINO
Still!

PAPAGENO
Ihr seht, dass ich nicht soll—

TAMINO
Still!

TAMINO *(aside)*
  The wise man considers and rejects
  what the common people say.

THE THREE LADIES
  They say whoever swears to their Brotherhood
  is condemned to hell, body and soul.

PAPAGENO
  The devil it would, outrageous!
  Tell me, Tamino, is that true?

TAMINO
  The invention of hypocrites,
  repeated by gossiping women.

PAPAGENO
  But the Queen says so too.

TAMINO
  She is a woman, and thinks like one.
  Be quiet, accept my word,
  think of your duty and use your head.

THE THREE LADIES *(to Tamino)*
  Why are you so unfriendly to us?

(Tamino courteously indicates that he is not allowed to speak.)

Papageno is saying nothing either. Speak up!

PAPAGENO *(to the Ladies, furtively)*
  I'd like to – but—

TAMINO
  Quiet!

PAPAGENO
  You see that I'm not allowed—

TAMINO
  Quiet!

TAMINO und PAPAGENO
Dass du/ich nicht kannst/kann das Plaudern lassen,
ist wahrlich eine Schand' für dich/mich!

ALLE FÜNF
Wir/sie müssen sie/uns mit Scham verlassen:
es plaudert keiner sicherlich!
Von festem Geiste ist ein Mann,
er denket, was er sprechen kann.

(Die Damen wollen gehen; die Eingeweihten schreien von innen.)

CHOR DER PRIESTER
Entweiht ist die heilige Schwelle!
Hinab mit den Weibern zur Hölle!

(Donner, Blitz und Schlag: zugleich zwei starke Donner)

DIE DREI DAMEN
O weh! O weh! O weh!

(stürzen in die Versenkung)

PAPAGENO *(fällt zu Boden)*
O weh! O weh! O weh!

(Dann fängt der dreimalige Akkord an.)

Sechster Auftritt

Tamino, Papageno, Sprecher, zweiter Priester mit Fackeln

SPRECHER
Heil dir, Jüngling! Dein standhaft männliches Betragen hat ge-
siegt. Zwar hast du noch manch rauhen und gefährlichen Weg zu
wandern, den du aber durch Hülfe der Götter glücklich endigen
wirst. Wir wollen also mit reinem Herzen unsere Wanderschaft
weiter fortsetzen.

(Er gibt ihm den Sack um.)

So! Nun komm.

(ab)

TAMINO and PAPAGENO
   The fact that you/I can't stop blabbing,
   is a shame for you/me.

ALL FIVE
   We/they must leave you/us defeated;
   no one is going to talk!
   A man is strong in spirit
   who thinks before he speaks.

(The Ladies are about to leave when the Initiates call out from within.)

CHORUS OF PRIESTS
   The holy sanctuary has been profaned;
   send these women down to hell!

(thunder and lightning: two loud thunderclaps)

THE THREE LADIES
   Alas! Alas! Alas!

(descend through the trapdoor)

PAPAGENO *(collapses on the ground)*
   Alas! Alas! Alas!

(Then the three chords are heard.)

Scene 6

Tamino, Papageno, Speaker, Second Priest with torches.

SPEAKER
   Hail to you, young man! Your steadfast, manly conduct has
   triumphed. It is true that you still have a long, harsh and dange-
   rous path to follow, but with the gods' help you will successful-
   ly complete it. Therefore let us with a pure heart continue on
   our way.

(He puts the sack on him.)

   So! Now come.

(They go out.)

ZWEITER PRIESTER
Was seh' ich! Freund, stehe auf! Wie ist dir?

PAPAGENO
Ich lieg' in einer Ohnmacht!

ZWEITER PRIESTER
Auf! Sammle dich und sei ein Mann!

PAPAGENO *(steht auf)*
Aber sagt mir nur, meine lieben Herren, warum muss ich denn alle die
Qualen und Schrecken empfinden? Wenn mir ja die Götter eine Papa-
gena bestimmten, warum denn mit so vielen Gefahren sie erringen?

ZWEITER PRIESTER
Diese neugierige Frage mag deine Vernunft dir beantworten.
Komm! Meine Pflicht heischt dich weiterzuführen.

(Er gibt ihm den Sack um.)

PAPAGENO
Bei so einer ewigen Wanderschaft möcht' einem wohl die Liebe
auf immer vergehen.

(ab)

Siebenter Auftritt

*Das Theater verwandelt sich in einen angenehmen Garten; Bäume, die
nach Art eines Hufeisens gesetzt sind; in der Mitte steht eine Laube
von Blumen und Rosen, worin Pamina schläft. Der Mond beleuchtet
ihr Gesicht. Ganz vorn steht eine Rasenbank. Monostatos kommt,
setzt sich nach einer Pause.*

MONOSTATOS
Ha, da find' ich ja die spröde Schöne! Und um so einer geringen
Pflanze wegen wollte man meine Fußsohlen behämmern? Also
bloß dem heutigen Tage hab' ich's zu verdanken, dass ich noch mit
heiler Haut auf die Erde trete. Hm! Was war denn eigentlich mein
Verbrechen? Dass ich mich in eine Blume vergaffte, die auf fremden
Boden versetzt war? Und welcher Mensch, wenn er auch von gelin-
derm Himmelstrich daher wanderte, würde bei so einem Anblick

SECOND PRIEST
What's this, friend, stand up! What's the matter with you?

PAPAGENO
I've fainted!

SECOND PRIEST
Up! Pull yourself together and be a man!

PAPAGENO *(stands)*
But just tell me, dear sirs, why I have to take all this anguish and fear? If the gods really have reserved a Papagena for me, why do I have to go through all these dangers to win her?

SECOND PRIEST
Let your reason provide the answer to this prying question. Come! My task is to lead you onwards.

(He puts the sack on him.)

PAPAGENO
An endless journey like this would make you want to give up love for ever.

(They go out.)

Scene 7

The scene changes to a pleasant garden; trees are positioned in a horseshoe; in the centre is a bower of flowers and roses, with Pamina asleep inside. The moon is shining on her face. Right at the front is a grassy bank. Monastato enters and after a pause sits down.

MONOSTATOS
So here is the untouchable beauty! And was it for such a slender plant that they wanted to beat the soles of my feet? So I have today to thank for still being able to tread the earth with undamaged feet. Hm! So what was it exactly that I did wrong? That I fell for a blossom that had strayed on to foreign soil? And what man, even if he had come here from milder climes, would remain cold and insensitive at

kalt und unempfindlich bleiben? Bei allen Sternen! das Mädchen wird noch um meinen Verstand mich bringen. Das Feuer, das in mir glimmt, wird mich noch verzehren.

(Er sieht sich allenthalben um.)

Wenn ich wüsste – dass ich so ganz allein und unbelauscht wäre – ich wagte es noch einmal.

(Er macht sich Wind mit beiden Händen.)

Es ist doch eine verdammte närrische Sache um die Liebe! Ein Küsschen, dächte ich, ließe sich entschuldigen.

Nr. 13 Arie

(Alles wird so piano gesungen und gespielt, als wenn die Musik in weiter Entfernung wäre.)

MONOSTATOS
Alles fühlt der Liebe Freuden,   [13]
schnäbelt, tändelt, herzet, küsst –
Und ich soll die Liebe meiden,
weil ein Schwarzer hässlich ist!
Ist mir denn kein Herz gegeben,
bin ich nicht von Fleisch und Blut?
Immer ohne Weibchen leben
wäre wahrlich Höllenglut.

Drum so will ich, weil ich lebe,
schnäbeln, küssen, zärtlich sein!
Lieber, guter Mond – vergebe,
eine Weiße nahm mich ein!
Weiß ist schön! – Ich muss sie küssen.
Mond! Verstecke dich dazu! –
Sollt es dich zu sehn verdrießen,
o so mach die Augen zu!

(Er schleicht langsam und leise hin.)

such a sight? By all the stars, the girl will drive me out of my mind. The fire that's smouldering within me is going to burn me up.

(He looks around on all sides.)

If I knew that I were completely alone and no one was listening, I'd try it again.

(He fans himself with both hands.)

Love is such a foolish thing! I think a little kiss would be forgiven.

No. 13 Aria

(Everything is sung and played as quietly as if the music were coming from far away.)

MONOSTATOS
Everyone feels the joys of love,   [13]
coos, flirts, cuddles and kisses;
and should I shun love
because a black man is ugly?
Don't I have a heart?
Am I not made of flesh and blood?
To live for ever without women
would be truly hellish pain.

So, since I'm alive, I want
to coo, kiss and be tender!
Dear, kind moon – forgive me:
her whiteness has bewitched me!
White is lovely! I have to kiss her.
Moon, hide yourself away!
If this is too much for you,
then close your eyes!

(Slowly and softly he creeps over.)

Achter Auftritt

Vorige, die Königin der Nacht kommt unter Donner aus der mittlern Versenkung, und so, dass sie gerade vor Pamina zu stehen kommt.

KÖNIGIN DER NACHT
   Zurück!

PAMINA *(erwacht)*
   Ihr Götter!

MONOSTATOS *(prallt zurück)*
   O weh! Das ist, wo ich nicht irre, die Göttin der Nacht.

(steht ganz still)

PAMINA
   Mutter! Mutter! Meine Mutter!

(Sie fällt ihr in die Arme.)

MONOSTATOS
   Mutter? Hm! Das muss man von weitem belauschen.

(schleicht ab)

KÖNIGIN DER NACHT
   Verdank es der Gewalt, mit der man dich mir entriss, dass ich noch deine Mutter mich nenne. Wo ist der Jüngling, den ich an dich sandte?

PAMINA
   Ach Mutter, der ist der Welt und den Menschen auf ewig entzogen. Er hat sich den Eingeweihten gewidmet.

KÖNIGIN DER NACHT
   Den Eingeweihten? Unglückliche Tochter, nun bist du auf ewig mir entrissen.

PAMINA
   Entrissen? O fliehen wir, liebe Mutter! Unter deinem Schutz trotz ich jeder Gefahr.

Scene 8

The above, to the sound of thunder the Queen of the Night emerges from the middle trapdoor and so appears standing right in front of Pamina.

QUEEN OF THE NIGHT
Stand back!

PAMINA *(awakening)*
You gods!

MONOSTATOS *(springing back)*
Alas! That is, unless I'm mistaken, the Queen of the Night.

(stands completely still)

PAMINA
Mother, mother, my mother!

(falls into her arms)

MONOSTATOS
Mother? Hm! I need to listen in from a distance.

(creeps away)

QUEEN OF THE NIGHT
If I still call myself your mother, you owe it to the violence with which you were wrenched from me. Where is the young man I sent to you?

PAMINA
Alas, mother, he has left the world and humanity behind for ever. He has joined the Initiates.

QUEEN OF THE NIGHT
The Initiates? Unhappy daughter, now you are lost to me for ever.

PAMINA
Lost? Oh, let's flee, my beloved mother! With you to protect me I defy every danger.

177

KÖNIGIN DER NACHT

Schutz? Liebes Kind, deine Mutter kann dich nicht mehr schützen. Mit deines Vaters Tod ging meine Macht zu Grabe.

PAMINA

Mein Vater—

KÖNIGIN DER NACHT

Übergab freiwillig den siebenfachen Sonnenkreis den Eingeweihten; diesen mächtigen Sonnenkreis trägt Sarastro auf seiner Brust. Als ich ihn darüber beredete, so sprach er mit gefalteter Stirne: „Weib! Meine letzte Stunde ist da – alle Schätze, so ich allein besaß, sind dein und deiner Tochter." – „Der alles verzehrende Sonnenkreis", fiel ich hastig ihm in die Rede – „ist den Geweihten bestimmt", antwortete er: „Sarastro wird ihn so männlich verwalten, wie ich bisher. Und nun kein Wort weiter; forsche nicht nach Wesen, die dem weiblichen Geiste unbegreiflich sind. Deine Pflicht ist, dich und deine Tochter der Führung weiser Männer zu überlassen."

PAMINA

Liebe Mutter, nach allem dem zu schließen, ist wohl auch der Jüngling auf immer für mich verloren.

KÖNIGIN DER NACHT

Verloren, wenn du nicht, eh' die Sonne die Erde färbt, ihn durch diese unterirdische Gewölbe zu fliehen beredest. Der erste Schimmer des Tages entscheidet, ob er ganz Dir oder den Eingeweihten gegeben sei.

PAMINA

Liebe Mutter, dürft' ich den Jüngling als Eingeweihten denn nicht auch ebenso zärtlich lieben, wie ich ihn jetzt liebe? Mein Vater selbst war ja mit diesen weisen Männern verbunden; er sprach jederzeit mit Entzücken von ihnen, preise ihre Güte – ihren Verstand – ihre Tugend. Sarastro ist nicht weniger tugendhaft.

KÖNIGIN DER NACHT

Was hör ich! Du meine Tochter, könntest die schändlichen Gründe dieser Barbaren verteidigen? So einen Mann lieben, der mit meinem Todfeinde verbunden, mit jedem Augenblick mir mei-

QUEEN OF THE NIGHT

Protect? Dear child, your mother can no longer protect you. When your father died, all my power was destroyed.

PAMINA

My father—

QUEEN OF THE NIGHT

He chose to hand the sevenfold circle of the sun over to the Initiates; Sarastro wears this mighty circle of the sun on his chest. As I was talking to him about it, his brow was furrowed and he said: 'My wife, my last hour has come. All the treasures that I alone possessed are now yours and your daughter's.' I quickly mentioned the all-consuming circle of the sun. 'It is destined for the Initiates,' he answered. 'Sarastro will control it as manfully as I have up until now. And now, not another word; do not try to understand things that are beyond a woman's grasp. Your duty is for you and your daughter to submit to the guidance of wise men.'

PAMINA

Beloved mother, as well as all that, now the young man is lost to me for ever.

QUEEN OF THE NIGHT

Lost, unless you, before the sun rises on this day, persuade him to flee these subterranean vaults. The first gleam of daylight will decide whether he belongs entirely to you or to the Initiates.

PAMINA

Beloved mother, may I not love the young man as tenderly when he is an Initiate as I do now? My father himself was associated with these men too, and always spoke of them with delight; he praised their kindness, their understanding, their virtue.

QUEEN OF THE NIGHT

What do I hear? Could you, my daughter, defend the shameful philosophy of these savages? To love such a man who is joined to my mortal enemies, who at every moment would be planning

nen Sturz bereiten würde? Siehst du hier diesen Stahl? Er ist für Sarastro geschliffen. Du wirst ihn töten, und den mächtigen Sonnenkreis mir überliefern.

PAMINA
Aber liebste Mutter—

KÖNIGIN DER NACHT
Kein Wort!

Nr. 14 Arie

KÖNIGIN DER NACHT
Der Hölle Rache kocht in meinem Herzen,   [14]
Tod und Verzweiflung flammet um mich her!
Fühlt nicht durch dich Sarastro Todesschmerzen,
so bist du meine Tochter nimmermehr:

Verstoßen sei auf ewig, verlassen sei auf ewig,
zertrümmert sei'n auf ewig alle Bande der Natur,
Wenn nicht durch dich Sarastro wird erblassen! –
Hört, Rachegötter! – Hört der Mutter Schwur.

(*Sie versinkt.*)

Neunter Auftritt

Pamina mit dem Dolch in der Hand

PAMINA
Morden soll ich? Götter! Das kann ich nicht! Das kann ich nicht!

(*steht in Gedanken*)

Zehnter Auftritt

Vorige, Monostatos.

MONOSTATOS (*kommt schnell, heimlich, und sehr freudig*)
Sarastros Sonnenkreis hat also auch seine Wirkung? Und diesen zu erhalten, soll das schöne Mädchen ihn morden? Das ist Salz in meine Suppe!

my downfall? Do you see this blade here? It has been sharpened
for Sarastro. You are going to kill him, and bring the mighty circle of the sun to me.

PAMINA
But, beloved mother—

QUEEN OF THE NIGHT
Not another word!

No. 14 Aria

QUEEN OF THE NIGHT
My heart is on fire with the vengeance of hell;   [14]
death and despair blaze all around me!
Unless Sarastro suffers death at your hands,
you will never be my daughter again.

Be cast out and abandoned for ever,
all ties of nature destroyed for ever,
unless Sarastro dies at your hands!
Hear, gods of vengeance, hear a mother's vow!

(She descends.)

Scene 9

Pamina with the dagger in her hand

PAMINA
Am I to commit murder? Gods! I cannot do that. I cannot do
that!

(lost in thought)

Scene 10

The above, Monostatos

MONOSTATOS *(hurries in secretly, overjoyed)*
So does Sarastro's circle of the sun have a power too? And to get
hold of it, does the pretty girl have to kill him? That's the icing
on the cake!

PAMINA

Aber schwur sie nicht bei allen Göttern, mich zu verstoßen, wenn ich den Dolch nicht gegen Sarastro kehre? Götter! Was soll ich nun?

MONOSTATOS

Dich mir anvertrauen!

(*nimmt ihr den Dolch*)

PAMINA (*erschrickt und schreit*)

Ha!

MONOSTATOS

Warum zitterst du? Vor meiner schwarzen Farbe, oder vor dem ausgedachten Mord?

PAMINA (*schüchtern*)

Du weißt also?

MONOSTATOS

Alles. Ich weiß sogar, dass nicht nur dein, sondern auch deiner Mutter Leben in meiner Hand steht. Ein einziges Wort sprech' ich zu Sarastro, und deine Mutter wird in diesem Gewölbe, in eben dem Wasser, das die Eingeweihten reinigen soll, wie man sagt, ersäuft. Aus diesem Gewölbe kommt sie nun sicher nicht mehr mit heiler Haut, wenn ich es will. Du hast also nur einen Weg, dich und deine Mutter zu retten.

PAMINA

Der wäre?

MONOSTATOS

Mich zu lieben.

PAMINA (*zitternd, für sich*)

Götter!

MONOSTATOS (*freudig*)

Das junge Bäumchen jagt der Sturm auf meine Seite. – Nun Mädchen! Ja, oder nein!

PAMINA

But did she not swear by all the gods to cast me out if I don't turn the dagger against Sarastro? Gods! What should I now do?

MONOSTATOS

Place your trust in me!

(takes the dagger away from her)

PAMINA *(cries in fright)*

Ha!

MONOSTATOS

What are you afraid of? My blackness, or your murderous intent?

PAMINA *(timidly)*

Then you know?

MONOSTATOS

Everything. I even know that not just your life is in my hands, but your mother's as well. Just one word to Sarastro from me and your mother will be drowned here in this vault in the very water where, so they say, the Initiates are to be purified. She will surely not now escape this vault unscathed, if I so choose. There is only one way you can save yourself and your mother.

PAMINA

What would that be?

MONOSTATOS

To love me.

PAMINA *(in fear, aside)*

Gods!

MONOSTATOS *(cheerfully)*

The storm pushes the young sapling over towards me. Now, girl! Yes or no?

PAMINA *(entschlossen)*
Nein!

MONOSTATOS *(voll Zorn)*
Nein? Und warum? Weil ich die Farbe eines schwarzen Gespensts trage? Nicht? Ha so stirb!

(Er ergreift sie bei der Hand.)

PAMINA
Monostatos, sieh mich hier auf meinen Knien – schone meiner!

MONOSTATOS
Liebe oder Tod! – Sprich! Dein Leben steht auf der Spitze.

PAMINA
Mein Herz hab ich dem Jüngling geopfert.

MONOSTATOS
Was kümmert mich dein Opfer. – Sprich!

PAMINA *(entschlossen)*
Nie!

Elfter Auftritt

Vorige, Sarastro.

MONOSTATOS
So fahr denn hin!

(Sarastro hält ihn schnell ab.)

Herr, mein Unternehmen ist nicht strafbar; man hat deinen Tod geschworen, darum wollt ich dich rächen.

SARASTRO
Ich weiß nur allzuviel. Weiß, dass deine Seele eben so schwarz als dein Gesicht ist. Auch würde ich dies schwarze Unternehmen mit höchster Strenge an dir bestrafen, wenn nicht ein böses Weib, das zwar eine sehr gute Tochter hat, den Dolch dazu geschmiedet hätte. Verdank es der bösen Handlung des Weibes, dass du ungestraft davon ziehst. Geh!

PAMINA *(firmly)*
No!

MONOSTATOS *(enraged)*
No? And why not? Because I am the colour of a black phantom? Is that it? Then die!

(He seizes her by the hand.)

PAMINA
Monostatos, see me on my knees – spare me!

MONOSTATOS
Love or death! Speak! Your life hangs in the balance.

PAMINA
I have sacrificed my heart to the young man.

MONOSTATOS
What do I care about your sacrifice? Speak!

PAMINA *(firmly)*
Never!

Scene 11

The above, Sarastro.

MONOSTATOS
Then die!

(Sarastro quickly stops him.)

Sir, I have done nothing wrong; they swore to kill you, and I wanted to avenge you.

SARASTRO
I know only too well. I know that your soul is just as black as your face. I would also punish you most severely for this black deed if it were not for the fact that an evil woman, who has a daughter of great goodness, forged the dagger for it. It is thanks to the woman's evil doings that you escape unpunished. Go!

MONOSTATOS *(im Abgehen)*
Jetzt such' ich die Mutter auf, weil die Tochter mir nicht beschieden ist.

(ab)

Zwölfter Auftritt

Vorige, ohne Monostatos.

PAMINA
Herr, strafe meine Mutter nicht, der Schmerz über meine Abwesenheit—

SARASTRO
Ich weiß alles. Weiß, dass sie in unterirdischen Gemächern des Tempels herumirrt, und Rache über mich und die Menschheit kocht. Allein, du sollst sehen, wie ich mich an deiner Mutter räche. Der Himmel schenke nur dem holden Jüngling Mut und Standhaftigkeit in seinem frommen Vorsatz, dann bist du mit ihm glücklich, und deine Mutter soll beschämt nach ihrer Burg zurückkehren.

Nr. 15 Arie

SARASTRO
In diesen heil'gen Hallen   [15]
kennt man die Rache nicht!
Und ist ein Mensch gefallen,
führt Liebe hin zur Pflicht.
Dann wandelt er an Freundes Hand
vergnügt und froh ins bess're Land.

In diesen heil'gen Mauern,
wo Mensch den Menschen liebt –
kann kein Verräter lauern,
weil man dem Feind vergibt.
Wen solche Lehren nicht erfreu'n,
verdienet nicht, ein Mensch zu sein.

(Beide gehen ab.)

MONOSTATOS *(as he leaves)*
Now I'll go and look for the mother, since the daughter is not for me.

(exit)

Scene 12

The above, without Monostatos.

PAMINA
Sir, do not punish my mother; her pain at my absence—

SARASTRO
I know everything. I know that she is roaming the subterranean chambers of the Temple, and is planning vengeance against me and humanity; but you will see how I take vengeance on your mother. May Heaven now send the gracious youth courage and fortitude in his devout intent, then you will be happy with him, and your mother will return in shame to her castle.

No. 15 Aria

SARASTRO
Within these sacred halls [15]
vengeance is unknown.
And if a person falls,
love guides him to his duty.
Then, led by the hand of friendship,
in joy and contentment he enters a better land.

Within these sacred walls
where people love one another,
there can be no traitors,
for we forgive our enemies.
Those who resist this teaching
are not worthy to belong to mankind.

(Both leave.)

Dreizehnter Auftritt

Das Theater verwandelt sich in eine Halle, wo das Flugwerk gehen kann. Das Flugwerk ist mit Rosen und Blumen umgeben, wo sich sodann eine Türe öffnet.

Tamino und Papageno werden ohne Säcke von den zwei Priestern hereingeführt. Ganz vorne sind zwei Rasenbänke.

SPRECHER
Hier seid ihr euch beide allein überlassen. Sobald die röchelnde Posaune tönt, dann nehmt ihr euren Weg dahin. Prinz, lebt wohl! Wir sehen uns, eh' ihr ganz am Ziele seid. Noch einmal, vergesst das Wort nicht: Schweigen.

(ab)

ZWEITER PRIESTER
Papageno, wer an diesem Ort sein Stillschweigen bricht, den strafen die Götter durch Donner und Blitz. Leb wohl!

(ab)

Vierzehnter Auftritt

Tamino, Papageno.

Tamino setzt sich auf eine Rasenbank.

PAPAGENO *(nach einer Pause)*
Tamino!

TAMINO *(verweisend)*
St!

PAPAGENO
Das ist ein lustiges Leben! Wär' ich lieber in meiner Strohhütte oder im Walde, so hört' ich doch manchmal einen Vogel pfeifen.

TAMINO *(verweisend)*
St!

Scene 13

The scene changes to a hall, where the flying machine can be used. The machine is adorned with roses and flowers, where a door then opens.

Tamino and Papageno, not wearing the sacks, are led in by the two priests. Downstage, two grassy banks.

SPEAKER
Here you will both be left alone. As soon as the rasp of the trombone rings out, continue on your way. Prince, farewell! We shall meet again before you reach your goal. Once again, do not forget the rule: silence.

(exit)

SECOND PRIEST
Papageno, those who break the silence here are punished by the gods with thunder and lightning. Farewell!

(exit)

Scene 14

Tamino, Papageno.

Tamino sits down on a grassy bank.

PAPAGENO *(after a pause)*
Tamino!

TAMINO *(reproachfully)*
Shh!

PAPAGENO
This is a lot of fun! I'd rather be in my straw hut, or in the woods, where at least I'd hear a bird sing from time to time.

TAMINO *(reproachfully)*
Shh!

PAPAGENO
Mit mir selbst werd' ich wohl sprechen dürfen; und auch wir zwei können zusammen sprechen: wir sind ja Männer.

TAMINO (*verweisend*)
St!

PAPAGENO (*singt*)
Lalala – lalala! Nicht einmal einen Tropfen Wasser bekommt man bei diesen Leuten, viel weniger sonst was.

Fünfzehnter Auftritt

Vorige, ein altes hässliches Weib kommt aus der Versenkung, hält auf einer Tasse einen großen Becher mit Wasser.

PAPAGENO (*sieht sie lang an*)
Ist das für mich?

WEIB
Ja, mein Engel!

PAPAGENO (*sieht sie wieder an, trinkt*)
Nicht mehr und nicht weniger als Wasser. Sag du mir, du unbekannte Schöne! Werden alle fremde Gäste auf diese Art bewirtet?

WEIB
Freilich, mein Engel!

PAPAGENO
So, so! Auf die Art werden die Fremden auch nicht gar zu häufig kommen.

WEIB
Sehr wenig.

PAPAGENO
Kann mir's denken. Geh, Alte, setze dich her zu mir, mir ist die Zeit verdammt lange. Sag du mir, wie alt bist du denn?

WEIB
Wie alt?

PAPAGENO
I'll just have to talk to myself; and the two of us can talk to each other – we're men, after all.

TAMINO *(reproachfully)*
Shh!

PAPAGENO *(sings)*
Lalala, lalala! These people don't even give you a drop of water, let alone anything else.

Scene 15

An ugly old woman comes out of the trapdoor, holding a tray with a large tumbler of water.

PAPAGENO *(takes a long look at her)*
Is that for me?

WOMAN
Yes, my angel!

PAPAGENO *(looks at her again, then drinks)*
Nothing more and nothing less than water. Tell me, you unknown beauty, are all visiting guests served this way?

WOMAN
They certainly are, my angel!

PAPAGENO
Aha! You probably don't get very many visitors then.

WOMAN
Very few.

PAPAGENO
I can imagine. Come on, old lady, sit down here beside me – I've got plenty to time on my hands. Tell me, how old are you, then?

WOMAN
How old?

PAPAGENO
Ja!

WEIB
Achtzehn Jahr und zwei Minuten.

PAPAGENO
Achtzehn Jahr und zwei Minuten?

WEIB
Ja!

PAPAGENO
Ha ha ha! Ei du junger Engel! Hast du auch einen Geliebten?

WEIB
I' freilich!

PAPAGENO
Ist er auch so jung wie du?

WEIB
Nicht gar, er ist um zehn Jahre älter.

PAPAGENO
Um zehn Jahr ist er älter als du? Das muss eine Liebe sein! Wie nennt sich denn dein Liebhaber?

WEIB
Papageno!

PAPAGENO *(erschrickt, Pause)*
Papageno? Wo ist er denn, dieser Papageno?

WEIB
Da sitzt er, mein Engel!

PAPAGENO
Ich wär' dein Geliebter?

WEIB
Ja, mein Engel!

PAPAGENO
Yes!

WOMAN
Eighteen years and two minutes.

PAPAGENO
Eighteen years and two minutes?

WOMAN
Yes!

PAPAGENO
Ha ha ha! Well, you young angel! Do you have a boyfriend too?

WOMAN
I certainly do!

PAPAGENO
Is he as young as you?

WOMAN
Not quite: he's about ten years older.

PAPAGENO
About ten years older than you? That must be true love! So what's your boyfriend called?

WOMAN
Papageno!

PAPAGENO *(takes fright, pause)*
Papageno? So where is this Papageno?

WOMAN
He's sitting right there, my angel!

PAPAGENO
Might I be your boyfriend?

WOMAN
Yes, my angel!

PAPAGENO *(nimmt schnell das Wasser und spritzt sie ins Gesicht)*
Sag du mir, wie heißt du denn?

WEIB
Ich heiße—

(starker Donner, die Alte hinkt schnell ab)

PAPAGENO
O weh!

(Tamino steht auf, droht ihm mit dem Finger.)

Nun sprech' ich kein Wort mehr!

Sechzehnter Auftritt

Die drei Knaben kommen in einem mit Rosen bedeckten Flugwerk. In der Mitte steht ein schöner gedeckter Tisch. Der eine hat die Flöte, der andere das Kästchen mit Glöckchen.

Nr. 16 Terzett

DIE DREI KNABEN
Seid uns zum zweiten Mal willkommen,   [16]
ihr Männer, in Sarastros Reich! –
Er schickt, was man euch abgenommen,
die Flöte und die Glöckchen euch.

Wollt ihr die Speisen nicht verschmähen,
so esset, trinket froh davon! –
Wenn wir zum dritten Mal uns sehen,
ist Freude eures Mutes Lohn!

Tamino Mut! Nah ist das Ziel!
Du, Papageno! Schweige still.

(Unter dem Terzett setzen sie den Tisch in die Mitte, und fliegen auf.)

PAPAGENO *(quickly takes the water and splashes his face)*
   Tell me, what are you called, then?

WOMAN
   I'm called—

(loud thunder, the old woman hobbles off)

PAPAGENO
   Oh, no!

(Tamino stands, and waves a threatening finger at him.)

   I'll certainly keep my mouth shut now!

Scene 16

The Three Boys arrive in a rose-covered flying machine. In the middle is a beautifully laid table. One of the boys has the flute, the other two the box with the bells.

No. 16 Trio

THE THREE BOYS
   Men, we welcome you a second time   [16]
   into Sarastro's realm!
   We return the things taken from you,
   the flute and the bells.

   If you do not spurn this fare,
   then happily eat and drink it!
   When you see us the third time,
   your courage will be rewarded by joy!

   Be brave, Tamino! The goal is close!
   You, Papageno, keep silent!

(During the trio they place the table in the centre, then fly off.)

Siebzehnter Auftritt

Tamino, Papageno

PAPAGENO
Tamino, wollen wir nicht speisen?

(Tamino bläst auf seiner Flöte.)

Blase du nur fort auf deiner Flöte, ich will meine Brocken blasen.
Herr Sarastro führt eine gute Küche. Auf die Art, ja da will ich
schon schweigen, wenn ich immer solche gute Bissen bekomme.
Nun will ich sehen, ob auch der Keller so gut bestellt ist.

(Er trinkt.)

Ha! – Das ist Götterwein!

(Die Flöte schweigt.)

Achtzehnter Auftritt

Vorige, Pamina

PAMINA *(freudig)*
Tamino! Du hier? Gütige Götter! Dank euch, dass ihr mich diesen
Weg führtet. Ich hörte deine Flöte – und so lief ich pfeilschnell
dem Tone nach. Aber du bist traurig? Sprichst nicht eine Silbe
mit deiner Pamina?

TAMINO *(seufzt)*
Ah!

(winkt ihr fortzugehen)

PAMINA
Wie? Ich soll dich meiden? liebst du mich nicht mehr?

TAMINO *(seufzt)*
Ah!

(winkt wieder fort)

Scene 17

Tamino, Papageno

PAPAGENO
Tamino, shall we have something to eat?

(Tamino plays his flute.)

You play away on your flute; I mean to tuck in. Mr Sarastro keeps a good kitchen. If I always get such lovely things to eat, I'll happily keep silent. Now I'll find out if his cellar is as well stocked.

(He drinks.)

Ha! This is the wine of the gods!

(The flute stops playing.)

Scene 18

The above, Pamina

PAMINA *(joyfully)*
Tamino! You're here? Kindly gods, I thank you for leading me this way. I heard your flute and so I rushed towards the sound. But are you downcast? Won't you say a single word to your Pamina?

TAMINO *(sighs)*
Ah!

(waves her away)

PAMINA
What? Am I to leave you alone? Don't you love me any more?

TAMINO *(sighs)*
Ah!

(waves her away again)

PAMINA

Ich soll fliehen, ohne zu wissen, warum? Tamino, holder Jüngling! Hab ich dich beleidigt? O kränke mein Herz nicht noch mehr. Bei dir such ich Trost – Hilfe – und du kannst mein liebevolles Herz noch mehr kränken? Liebst du mich nicht mehr?

(Tamino seufzt.)

Papageno, sage du mir, sag, was ist mit meinem Freund?

(Papageno hat einen Brocken in dem Mund, hält mit beiden Händen die Speisen zu, winkt fortzugehen.)

PAMINA

Wie? auch du? Erkläre mir wenigstens die Ursache eures Stillschweigens.

PAPAGENO

St!

(Er deutet ihr fortzugehen.)

PAMINA

O das ist mehr als Kränkung – mehr als Tod!

(Pause)

Liebster, einziger Tamino!

Nr. 17 Arie

Ach ich fühls, es ist verschwunden!   [17]
Ewig hin der Liebe Glück! –
Nimmer kommt ihr Wonnestunden
meinem Herzen mehr zurück!

Sieh, Tamino! Diese Tränen
fließen, Trauter, dir allein,
fühlst du nicht der Liebe Sehnen –
so wird Ruh' im Tode sein!

(ab)

198

PAMINA

Am I to go away without knowing why? Tamino, gentle youth, have I offended you? Oh, do not grieve my heart once more. I seek consolation – help – from you and yet are you able to cause my loving heart more pain? Don't you love me any more?

(Tamino sighs.)

Papageno, you tell me, what is wrong with my friend?

(Papageno has his mouth full and food in both hands; he waves her away.)

PAMINA

What, you as well? At least tell me the reason for this silence.

PAPAGENO

Shh!

(He signals for her to go away.)

PAMINA

Oh, that is worse than an insult – worse than death!

(Pause)

My beloved, my only Tamino!

No. 17 Aria

Alas, I feel that it has vanished;   [17]
the happiness of love has gone for ever!
Hours of rapture, you will never
return to my heart.

See, Tamino, these tears
fall for you alone, my love.
If you do not feel the yearning of love,
then I shall find peace in death.

(exit)

Neunzehnter Auftritt

Tamino, Papageno.

PAPAGENO *(isst hastig)*
Nicht wahr Tamino, ich kann auch schweigen, wenn's sein muss.
– Ja, bei so einem Unternehmen da bin ich Mann.

(Er trinkt.)

Der Herr Koch, und der Herr Kellermeister sollen leben.

(dreimaliger Posaunenton, Tamino winkt Papageno, dass er gehen soll.)

Gehe du nur voraus, ich komm schon nach.

(Tamino will ihn mit Gewalt fortführen.)

Der Stärkere bleibt da!

(Tamino droht ihm, und geht rechts ab; ist aber links gekommen.)

Jetzt will ich mir's erst recht wohl sein lassen. Da ich in meinem
besten Appetit bin, soll ich gehen. Das lass' ich wohl bleiben. Ich
ging' jetzt nicht fort, und wenn Herr Sarastro seine sechs Löwen
an mich spannte.

(Die Löwen kommen heraus, er erschrickt.)

O Barmherzigkeit, ihr gütigen Götter! – Tamino, rette mich! Die
Herrn Löwen machen eine Mahlzeit aus mir.

*(Tamino bläst sein Flöte, kommt schnell zurück; die Löwen gehen
hinein. Tamino winkt ihm.)*

Ich gehe schon! Heiß du mich einen Schelmen, wenn ich dir nicht
in allem folge.

(dreimaliger Posaunenton)

Das geht uns an. – Wir kommen schon. – Aber hör einmal, Tamino,
was wird denn noch alles mit uns werden?

(Tamino deutet gen Himmel.)

Scene 19

Tamino, Papageno.

PAPAGENO *(eating hurriedly)*
You see, Tamino, I can keep silent too when I have to. I'm a real man when it comes to something like that.

(He drinks.)

Long live the chef and the cellarman.

(Three trombone chords. Tamino signals to Papageno that he has to go.)

You go on ahead, I'll be right behind you.

(Tamino tries to drag him away.)

The stronger man stays here!

(Tamino threatens him, and exits stage right, although he has entered from the left.)

Now I'll be left in peace. Just when I'm tucking in, am I supposed to go? I'll give that a miss. I'm not leaving, not even if Mr Sarastro hitched me up to his six lions.

(The lions appear, he takes fright.)

Oh, mercy, kindly gods! Tamino, save me! The lions are going to have me for supper.

(Tamino plays his flute and races back; the lions leave. Tamino signals to him.)

I'm just coming! You can call me a rogue if I don't follow you everywhere.

(Three trombone chords)

That's for us. We're just coming. But listen, Tamino, what's going to happen to us in the end?

(Tamino points to the sky.)

Die Götter soll ich fragen?

(Tamino deutet ja.)

Ja, die könnten uns freilich mehr sagen, als wir wissen!

(dreimaliger Posaunenton, Tamino reißt ihn mit Gewalt fort.)

Eile nur nicht so, wir kommen noch immer zeitlich genug, um uns braten zu lassen.

(ab)

Zwanzigster Auftritt

Das Theater verwandelt sich in das Gewölbe von Pyramiden.

Sarastro, Sprecher und einige Priester. Zwei Priester tragen eine beleuchtete Pyramide auf den Schultern; jeder Priester hat eine transparente Pyramide, in der Größe einer Laterne, in der Hand.

Nr. 18 Chor der Priester

CHOR

O Isis und Osiris, welche Wonne! [18]
Die düstre Nacht verscheucht der Glanz der Sonne! –
Bald fühlt der edle Jüngling neues Leben,
bald ist er unserm Dienste ganz gegeben.
Sein Geist ist kühn, sein Herz ist rein –
bald wird er unser würdig sein.

Einundzwanzigster Auftritt

Vorige, Tamino, der hereingeführt wird, später Pamina.

SARASTRO

Prinz, dein Betragen war bis hieher männlich und gelassen; nun hast du noch zwei gefährliche Wege zu wandern. Schlägt dein Herz noch ebenso warm für Pamina – und wünschest du einst als ein weiser Fürst zu regieren, so mögen die Götter dich ferner begleiten. Deine Hand... Man bringe Paminen!

Should I ask the gods?

(Tamino nods.)

Yes, they can certainly tell us more than we know!

(Three trombone chords, Tamino forcefully pulls him away.)

No need to hurry, we'll get there in plenty of time to be roasted.

(exeunt)

Scene 20

The scene changes to the vault of a pyramid.

Sarastro, the Speaker and some priests. Two priests are bearing an illuminated pyramid on their shoulders; each priest has a transparent pyramid the size of a lantern in his hand.

No. 18 Priests' Chorus

CHORUS

O Isis und Osiris, what joy!   [18]
The radiant sun banishes dark night.
Soon the noble youth will experience new life;
soon he will serve us completely.
His spirit is bold, his heart is pure,
soon he will be worthy of us.

Scene 21

The above, Tamino, who is led in, later Pamina.

SARASTRO

Prince, thus far your conduct has been manly and composed; now you have two further perilous paths to take. If your heart still beats as fondly for Pamina and if you wish to reign as a wise ruler one day, then may the gods lead you on. Your hand... Bring in Pamina!

(Eine Stille herrscht bei allen Priestern, Pamina wird mit eben diesem Sack, welcher die Eingeweihten bedeckt, hereingeführt, Sarastro löst die Bande am Sacke auf.)

PAMINA
Wo bin ich? Welch eine fürchterliche Stille! – Saget, wo ist mein Jüngling?

SARASTRO
Er wartet deiner, um dir das letzte Lebewohl zu sagen.

PAMINA
Das letzte Lebewohl! O wo ist er? Führe mich zu ihm!

SARASTRO
Hier!

PAMINA
Tamino!

TAMINO
Zurück!

Nr .19 Terzett

Sarastro, Pamina, Tamino

PAMINA
Soll ich dich, Teurer, nicht mehr sehn?   [19]

SARASTRO
Ihr werdet froh euch wiedersehn!

PAMINA
Dein warten tödliche Gefahren!

TAMINO
Die Götter mögen mich bewahren!

PAMINA
Dein warten tödliche Gefahren!

SARASTRO und TAMINO
Die Götter mögen ihn/mich bewahren!

(All the priests are silent; Pamina is led in wearing the same sack as was put on the Initiates; Sarastro undoes the ties on the sack.)

PAMINA
Where am I? What fearful silence! Tell me, where is my young man?

SARASTRO
He is waiting for you, to bid you a final farewell.

PAMINA
A final farewell! Where is he? Lead me to him!

SARASTRO
Here!

PAMINA
Tamino!

TAMINO
Stand back!

No. 19 Trio

Sarastro, Pamina, Tamino

PAMINA
My beloved, am I never to see you again?   [19]

SARASTRO
You will see each other again in joy.

PAMINA
Deadly dangers await you.

TAMINO
May the gods watch over me.

PAMINA
Deadly dangers await you.

SARASTRO and TAMINO
May the gods watch over him/me.

PAMINA
> Du wirst dem Tode nicht entgehen,
> mir flüstert Ahnung dieses ein!

SARASTRO und TAMINO
> Der Götter Wille mag geschehen;
> ihr Wink soll ihm/mir Gesetze sein!

PAMINA
> O liebtest du, wie ich dich liebe,
> du würdest nicht so ruhig sein!

SARASTRO und TAMINO
> Glaub mir, er fühlet/ich fühle gleiche Triebe,
> wird/werd' ewig dein Getreuer sein.

SARASTRO
> Die Stunde schlägt, nun müsst ihr scheiden!

TAMINO und PAMINA
> Wie bitter sind der Trennung Leiden!

SARASTRO
> Tamino muss nun wirklich fort!

TAMINO
> Pamina, ich muss nun wirklich fort!

PAMINA
> Tamino muss nun wieder fort!

SARASTRO
> Nun muss er fort!

TAMINO
> Nun muss ich fort!

PAMINA
> So musst du fort!

PAMINA und PAMINA
> Tamino/Pamina! Lebe wohl!

PAMINA
The thought that you will not
escape death troubles me!

SARASTRO and TAMINO
The gods' will be done;
let their bidding be his/my command.

PAMINA
If you loved me as I love you,
you would not be so calm.

SARASTRO and TAMINO
Believe me, he feels/I feel the same,
he/I will always be faithful to you.

SARASTRO
The time has come, you must part.

TAMINO and PAMINA
How bitter are the pains of parting!

SARASTRO
Tamino must go now once more!

TAMINO
Pamina, I must truly go now!

PAMINA
Tamino must truly go now!

SARASTRO
Now he must go!

TAMINO
Now I must go!

PAMINA
So you must go!

TAMINO and PAMINA
Pamina/Tamino, farewell!

SARASTRO
Nun eile fort!
Dich ruft dein Wort!
Die Stunde schlägt! Wir sehn uns wieder!

TAMINO und **PAMINA**
O goldne Ruhe! Kehre wieder!
Lebe wohl! Lebe wohl!

SARASTRO
Wir sehn uns wieder!

(entfernen sich)

Zweiundzwanzigster Auftritt

Papageno.

PAPAGENO *(von außen)*
Tamino! Tamino! willst du mich denn gänzlich verlassen?

(Er sucht herein.)

Wenn ich nur wenigstens wüsste, wo ich wäre – Tamino! – Tamino! Solang' ich lebe, bleib' ich nicht mehr von dir – nur diesmal verlass mich armen Reisegefährten nicht!

(Er kommt an die Türe, wo Tamino abgeführt worden ist.)

EINE STIMME *(ruft)*
Zurück!

(dann ein Donnerschlag, das Feuer schlägt zur Türe heraus; starker Akkord)

PAPAGENO
Barmherzige Götter! – Wo wend' ich mich hin? – Wenn ich nur wüsste, wo ich hereinkam.

(Er kommt an die Türe, wo er hereinkam.)

DIE STIMME
Zurück!

(Donner, Feuer und Akkord wie oben)

SARASTRO
Hurry on your way!
Your word calls you.
The time has come, we shall meet again!

TAMINO and PAMINA
Ah, may golden hours of peace return!
Farewell, farewell!

SARASTRO
We shall meet again!

(They go off.)

Scene 22

Papageno.

PAPAGENO *(offstage)*
Tamino! Tamino! Are you going to abandon me completely?

(He searches.)

If I knew at least where I was. Tamino! – Tamino! I'll never leave you again, as long as I live. Just this time don't abandon your companion!

(He comes to the door where Tamino was led off.)

A VOICE *(calls)*
Stand back!

(then a thunderclap; flames shoot out of the door; loud chord)

PAPAGENO
Merciful gods! Where can I turn? If I only knew where I came in from.

(He arrives at the door through which he came in.)

THE VOICE
Stand back!

(thunder, fire and the chord, as above)

PAPAGENO
Nun kann ich weder zurück, noch vorwärts!

(*weint*)

Muss vielleicht am Ende gar verhungern. Schon recht! Warum bin ich mitgereist?

Dreiundzwanzigster Auftritt

Vorige, Sprecher mit seiner Pyramide.

SPRECHER
Mensch! Du hättest verdient, auf immer in finstern Klüften der Erde zu wandern; die gütigen Götter aber entlassen der Strafe dich. Dafür aber wirst du das himmlische Vergnügen der Eingeweihten nie fühlen.

PAPAGENO
Je nun, es gibt ja noch mehr Leute meines Gleichen. Mir wäre jetzt ein gut Glas Wein das größte Vergnügen.

SPRECHER
Sonst hast du keinen Wunsch in dieser Welt?

PAPAGENO
Bis jetzt nicht.

SPRECHER
Man wird dich damit bedienen!

(*ab*)

(*Sogleich kommt ein großer Becher, mit rotem Wein angefüllt, aus der Erde.*)

PAPAGENO
Juchhe! Da ist er ja schon!

(*trinkt*)

Herrlich! Himmlisch! Göttlich! Ha! ich bin jetzt so vergnügt, dass ich bis zur Sonne fliegen wollte, wenn ich Flügel hätte. Ha! Mir wird ganz wunderlich ums Herz. Ich möchte – ich wünschte – ja was denn?

PAPAGENO

Now I can't go backwards or forwards!

(bursts into tears)

I'm going to end up starving to death. Serves me right! Why did I come along with him?

Scene 23

The above, the Speaker with his pyramid

SPEAKER

Man! You deserve to wander for ever in the dark bowels of the earth; but the kindly gods have spared you this punishment. Therefore you will never experience the divine joys of the Initiated.

PAPAGENO

Oh well, there are plenty more people like me. The greatest pleasure for me right now would be a nice glass of wine.

SPEAKER

Is there nothing else in this world you wish for?

PAPAGENO

Not so far.

SPEAKER

You will be served one!

(exit)

(Immediately out of the ground comes a large tumbler filled with red wine.)

PAPAGENO

Hurrah! That's a lovely sight!

(drinks)

Wonderful! Heavenly! Divine! I feel so happy now that I could fly up to the sun, if I had wings. Ha! I've got a lovely feeling in my heart. I would – I'd like to – well, what?

211

Nr. 20 Arie

(Er schlägt das Glockenspiel.)

PAPAGENO

Ein Mädchen oder Weibchen [20]
wünscht Papageno sich!
O so ein sanftes Täubchen
wär' Seligkeit für mich!
Dann schmeckte mir Trinken und Essen,
dann könnt' ich mit Fürsten mich messen,
des Lebens als Weiser mich freu'n,
und wie im Elysium sein.

Ein Mädchen oder Weibchen
wünscht Papageno sich!
O so ein sanftes Täubchen
wär' Seligkeit für mich!
Ach kann ich denn keiner von allen
den reizenden Mädchen gefallen?
Helf' eine mir nur aus der Not,
sonst gräm' ich mich wahrlich zu Tod.

Ein Mädchen oder Weibchen
wünscht Papageno sich!
O so ein sanftes Täubchen
wär' Seligkeit für mich!
Wird keine mir Liebe gewähren,
so muss mich die Flamme verzehren!
Doch küsst mich ein weiblicher Mund –
so bin ich schon wieder gesund.

Vierundzwanzigster Auftritt

Vorige, die Alte, tanzend, und auf ihren Stock dabei sich stützend.

WEIB

Da bin ich schon, mein Engel!

PAPAGENO

Du hast dich meiner erbarmt?

No. 20 Aria

(He plays along on the glockenspiel.)

PAPAGENO

A girl or little woman [20]
is what Papageno would like!
Such a tender little dove
would be bliss for me!
Then I'd enjoy eating and drinking,
I'd feel equal to a king,
I'd enjoy life like a wise man
and feel I was in heaven.

A girl or little woman
is what Papageno would like!
Such a tender little dove
would be bliss for me!
Is there really no pretty girl
I appeal to?
Let just one help me in my need;
otherwise I'll die of a broken heart.

A girl or little woman
is what Papageno would like!
Such a tender little dove
would be bliss for me!
If no one will offer me love
then the flame will surely kill me!
But a kiss from a woman's lips
would make me well again.

Scene 24

The above, the old Woman dances in, leaning on her stick.

WOMAN

Here I am, my angel!

PAPAGENO

Have you taken pity on me?

WEIB

Ja, mein Engel!

PAPAGENO

Das ist ein Glück!

WEIB

Und wenn du mir versprichst, mir ewig treu zu bleiben, dann sollst du sehen, wie zärtlich dein Weibchen dich lieben wird.

PAPAGENO

Ei du zärtliches Närrchen!

WEIB

O wie will ich dich umarmen, dich liebkosen, dich an mein Herz drücken!

PAPAGENO

Auch ans Herz drücken?

WEIB

Komm, reiche mir zum Pfand unsers Bundes deine Hand.

PAPAGENO

Nur nicht so hastig, lieber Engel! – So ein Bündnis braucht doch auch seine Überlegung.

WEIB

Papageno, ich rate dir, zaudre nicht. – Deine Hand, oder du bist auf immer hier eingekerkert.

PAPAGENO

Eingekerkert?

WEIB

Wasser und Brot wird deine tägliche Kost sein. Ohne Freund, ohne Freundin musst du leben, und der Welt auf immer entsagen.

PAPAGENO

Wasser trinken? Der Welt entsagen? Nein, da will ich doch lieber eine Alte nehmen, als gar keine. Nun, da hast du meine Hand, mit der Versicherung, dass ich dir immer getreu bleibe,

WOMAN
Yes, my angel!

PAPAGENO
That's good news!

WOMAN
And if you promise to be true to me for ever, then you'll see how tenderly your little wife will love you.

PAPAGENO
Oh, you silly old dear!

WOMAN
How I want to cuddle you, hug you and press you to my heart!

PAPAGENO
To your heart as well?

WOMAN
Come along, give me your hand to confirm that we are one.

PAPAGENO
Not so fast, my dear angel! A bond like that needs a bit of thought.

WOMAN
Papageno, I advise you not to hesitate. Your hand, or you'll be locked up here for eternity.

PAPAGENO
Locked up?

WOMAN
You'll have bread and water every day. You'll have to live without friends or girlfriends, and renounce the world for ever.

PAPAGENO
Drink water? Renounce the world? No, I'd rather have an old woman than none at all. There, you have my hand, with the assurance that I'll be true to you for ever,

(für sich)

solang' ich keine Schönere sehe.

WEIB
Das schwörst du?

PAPAGENO
Ja, das schwör' ich!

(Weib verwandelt sich in ein junges Weib, welches ebenso gekleidet ist, wie Papageno.)

PAPAGENO
Pa – Pa – Papagena!

(Er will sie umarmen.)

Fünfundzwanzigster Auftritt

Vorige, Sprecher nimmt sie hastig bei der Hand.

SPRECHER
Fort mit dir, junges Weib! Er ist deiner noch nicht würdig.

(Er schleppt sie hinein, Papageno will nach.)

Zurück, sag ich! oder zittre.

PAPAGENO
Eh' ich mich zurückziehe, soll die Erde mich verschlingen.

(Er sinkt hinab.)

O ihr Götter!

Sechsundzwanzigster Auftritt

Das Theater verwandelt sich in einen kurzen Garten.

Nr. 21 Finale

DIE DREI KNABEN *(fahren herunter)*
Bald prangt, den Morgen zu verkünden,   [21a]
die Sonn' auf goldner Bahn –

(aside)

as long as I don't find someone nicer.

WOMAN
Do you swear?

PAPAGENO
Yes, I swear!

*(She turns into a young woman, who is dressed exactly like
Papageno.)*

PAPAGENO
Pa – Pa – Papagena!

(He tries to embrace her.)

Scene 25

The above, the Speaker enters and quickly grabs Papagena by the hand.

SPEAKER
Away with you, young woman! He is not yet worthy of you.

(He drags her off; Papageno tries to follow.)

Stand back, I say! Or tremble.

PAPAGENO
The earth will have to swallow me before I stand back.

(He sinks down.)

O you gods!

Scene 26

The scene changes to a small garden.

No. 21 Finale

THE THREE BOYS *(descending from above)*
Soon the sun will shine down   [21a]
on its golden path to herald the day.

bald soll der Aberglaube schwinden,
bald siegt der weise Mann!
O holde Ruhe, steig hernieder,
kehr in der Menschen Herzen wieder.
Dann ist die Erd' ein Himmelreich
und Sterbliche den Göttern gleich.

ERSTER KNABE
Doch seht, Verzweiflung quält Paminen!

ZWEITER und DRITTER KNABE
Wo ist sie denn?

ERSTER KNABE
Sie ist von Sinnen!

ZWEITER und DRITTER KNABE
Sie quält verschmähter Liebe Leiden,
lasst uns der Armen Trost bereiten!
Fürwahr, ihr Schicksal geht uns nah!
O wäre nur ihr Jüngling da!
Sie kommt, lasst uns beiseite gehn,
damit wir, was sie mache, sehn.

(*gehen beiseite*)

Siebundzwanzigster Auftritt

Vorige, Pamina halb wahnwitzig mit einem Dolch in der Hand.

PAMINA *(zum Dolch)*
Du also bist mein Bräutigam –
durch dich vollend' ich meinen Gram!

DIE DREI KNABEN *(beiseite)*
Welch' dunkle Worte sprach sie da!
Die Arme ist dem Wahnsinn nah!

PAMINA
Geduld, mein Trauter, ich bin dein –
bald werden wir vermählet sein!

218

Superstition must soon vanish,
the wise man soon will triumph.
O lovely peace, descend;
return to human hearts;
then the earth will be a heavenly kingdom,
and mortals become like gods.

FIRST BOY
But look, Pamina is gripped by despair!

SECOND and THIRD BOY
Where is she, then?

FIRST BOY
She's losing her mind!

SECOND and THIRD BOY
She's in torment over her rejected love.
Let us console the poor girl.
Truly, her fate touches us.
If only her young man were here!
She's coming; let us stand aside,
so we can see what she does.

(They stand aside.)

Scene 27

The above, Pamina half-crazed, with a dagger in her hand.

PAMINA *(addressing the dagger)*
So you are my bridegroom,
through you I shall end my pain.

THE THREE BOYS *(aside)*
What dark words she has just uttered!
The poor girl has nearly lost her mind.

PAMINA
Patience, my beloved! I am yours;
soon we shall be united.

DIE DREI KNABEN *(beiseite)*
Wahnsinn tobt ihr im Gehirne –
Selbstmord steht auf ihrer Stirne!

(zu Pamina)

Holdes Mädchen, sieh uns an!

PAMINA
Sterben will ich, weil der Mann,
den ich nimmermehr kann hassen,
Seine Traute kann verlassen!

(auf den Dolch zeigend)

Dies gab meine Mutter mir.

DIE DREI KNABEN
Selbstmord strafet Gott an dir!

PAMINA
Lieber durch dies Eisen sterben,
als durch Liebesgram verderben.
Mutter, durch dich leide ich,
und dein Fluch verfolget mich!

DIE DREI KNABEN
Mädchen! Willst du mit uns gehn?

PAMINA
Ja, des Jammers Maß ist voll!
Falscher Jüngling, lebe wohl!
Sieh, Pamina stirbt durch dich!
Dieses Eisen töte mich!

(will sich erstechen)

DIE DREI KNABEN *(halten ihr den Arm)*
Ha, Unglückliche! Halt ein!
Sollte dies dein Jüngling sehen,
würde er für Gram vergehen,
denn er liebet dich allein.

THE THREE BOYS *(aside)*
Her mind is in turmoil;
suicide is written on her brow.

(to Pamina)

Fair maiden, look at us!

PAMINA
I wish to die, because the man
whom I can never hate
has abandoned his beloved.

(indicating the dagger)

My mother gave me this.

THE THREE BOYS
God will punish your suicide.

PAMINA
Better to die through this blade
than be destroyed by sorrow.
Mother, because of you I suffer,
and your curse pursues me.

THE THREE BOYS
Maiden, will you come with us?

PAMINA
Yes, my cup of misery is full!
False young man, farewell!
See, through you Pamina dies;
let this blade end my life.

(She makes a lunge.)

THE THREE BOYS *(holding her arm)*
Ha, stop, poor girl!
If your young man saw this
his sorrow would kill him;
for he loves no one but you.

221

PAMINA *(erholt sich)*
Was? Er fühlte Gegenliebe?
Und verbarg mir seine Triebe –
wandte sein Gesicht von mir?
Warum sprach er nicht mit mir?

DIE DREI KNABEN
Dieses müssen wir verschweigen,
doch wir wollen dir ihn zeigen,
und du wirst mit Staunen sehn,
Dass er dir sein Herz geweiht,
und den Tod für dich nicht scheut!

PAMINA
Führt mich hin, ich möcht ihn sehn.

DIE DREI KNABEN
Komm, wir wollen zu ihm gehn.

ALLE VIER
Zwei Herzen, die von Liebe brennen,
kann Menschenohnmacht niemals trennen –
verloren ist der Feinde Müh,
die Götter selbst beschützen sie.

(Sie gehen ab.)

Achtundzwanzigster Auftritt

Das Theater verwandelt sich in zwei große Berge; in dem einen ist ein Wasserfall, worin man Sausen und Brausen hört; der andre speit Feuer aus; jeder Berg hat ein durchbrochenes Gegitter, worin man Feuer und Wasser sieht; da, wo das Feuer brennt, muss der Horizont hellrot sein, und wo das Wasser ist, liegt schwarzer Nebel. Die Szenen sind Felsen, jede Szene schließt sich mit einer eisernen Türe.   [21b]

Tamino ist leicht angezogen ohne Sandalen. Zwei schwarz geharnischte Männer führen Tamino herein. Auf ihren Helmen brennt Feuer, sie lesen ihm die transparente Schrift vor, welche auf einer Pyramide geschrieben steht. Diese Pyramide steht in der Mitte ganz in der Höhe, nahe am Gegitter.

PAMINA *(recovers)*
What? He loves me in return?
Yet he kept his feelings from me,
turned his face away?
Why did he not speak to me?

THE THREE BOYS
We may not tell you this!
But we want to show you him
and you will be amazed to see
that his heart is devoted to you,
and for you he does not shrink from death.

PAMINA
Lead me on – I want to see him.

THE THREE BOYS
Come, let's go to him.

ALL FOUR
Two hearts that are aflame with love
cannot be kept apart by human frailty.
The enemy toils in vain;
for the gods themselves protect them.

(They leave.)

Scene 28

The scene changes to two tall mountains; on one is a waterfall that can be heard swishing and roaring; the other is spitting out fire; each has an open grille through which fire and water can be seen; where the fire burns, the horizon must be bright red, and where the water is hangs a dark mist. The stage cloths show rocks, each one with a closed iron door. [21b]

Tamino is lightly clothed, without sandals. Two men in black armour lead Tamino in. There is fire burning on their helmets. They read him the illuminated inscription that is written on one of the pyramids. This pyramid stands high up in the centre, near the grilles.

ERSTER und ZWEITER GEHARNISCHTER MANN
Der, welcher wandert diese Straße voll Beschwerden, [21]
wird rein durch Feuer, Wasser, Luft und Erden.
Wenn er des Todes Schrecken überwinden kann,
schwingt er sich aus der Erde himmelan!
Erleuchtet wird er dann im Stande sein,
sich den Mysterien der Isis ganz zu weih'n.

TAMINO
Mich schreckt kein Tod, als Mann zu handeln,
den Weg der Tugend fort zu wandeln!
Schließt mir des Schreckens Pforten auf –
ich wage froh den kühnen Lauf.

(will gehen)

PAMINA (von innen)
Tamino, halt! Ich muss dich sehn!

TAMINO
Was hör' ich? Paminens Stimme?

ERSTER und ZWEITER GEHARNISCHTE MANN
Ja, ja, das ist Paminens Stimme!

TAMINO und ERSTER und ZWEITE GEHARNISCHTE MANN
Wohl mir/dir, nun kann sie mit mir/dir gehn!
Nun trennet uns/euch kein Schicksal mehr,
wenn auch der Tod beschieden wär'!

TAMINO
Ist mir erlaubt, mit ihr zu sprechen?

ERSTER und ZWEITER GEHARNISCHTE MANN
Dir sei erlaubt, mit ihr zu sprechen.

TAMINO und ERSTER und ZWEITER GEHARNISCHTE MANN
Welch Glück, wenn wir uns/euch wiedersehn.
Froh Hand in Hand in Tempel gehn.
Ein Weib, das Nacht und Tod nicht scheut,
ist würdig, und wird eingeweiht.

224

FIRST and SECOND MAN IN ARMOUR
    The man who carries his burden along this path   [21c]
    is purified by fire, water, air and earth;
    if he can conquer the fear of death,
    he will ascend from earth into heaven.
    Enlightenment will then allow him
    to dedicate himself entirely to Isis.

TAMINO
    Death does not deflect me from being a man
    and following the path of virtue.
    Open wide the gates of terror!
    I happily venture on this intrepid path.

(making to go)

PAMINA *(from within)*
    Tamino, stop, I have to see you.

TAMINO
    Is that Pamina's voice I hear?

FIRST and SECOND MAN IN ARMOUR
    Yes, yes, that is Pamina's voice!

TAMINO and FIRST and SECOND MAN IN ARMOUR
    Happily she can now journey with me/you.
    No fate will separate us/you now,
    even if death awaits us/you.

TAMINO
    Am I permitted to speak to her?

FIRST and SECOND MAN IN ARMOUR
    You are permitted to speak to her.

TAMINO and FIRST and SECOND MAN IN ARMOUR
    What joy to see each other/you again,
    walking joyfully into the Temple hand in hand.
    A woman unafraid of night and death
    is worthy, and will join the Initiates.

(Die Türe wird aufgemacht, Tamino, Pamina umarmen sich.)

PAMINA
Tamino mein! O welch ein Glück!

TAMINO
Pamina mein! O welch ein Glück!
Hier sind die Schreckenspforten,
die Not und Tod mir dräun.

PAMINA
Ich werde aller Orten
an deiner Seite sein.
Ich selbsten führe dich –
die Liebe leite mich!

(Sie nimmt ihn bei der Hand.)

Sie mag den Weg mit Rosen streu'n,
weil Rosen stets bei Dornen sein.
Spiel du die Zauberflöte an,
sie schütze uns auf unsrer Bahn.
Es schnitt in einer Zauberstunde
mein Vater sie aus tiefstem Grunde
der tausendjähr'gen Eiche aus
bei Blitz und Donner, – Sturm und Braus.
Nun komm und spiel' die Flöte an!
Sie leite uns auf grauser Bahn.

PAMINA und TAMINO, ERSTER und ZWEITER
GEHARNISCHTE MANN
Wir wandeln/ihr wandelt durch des Tones Macht,
froh durch des Todes düstre Nacht.

(Die Türen werden nach ihnen zugeschlagen; man sieht Tamino und Pamina wandern; man hört Feuergeprassel und Windesgeheul, manchmal den Ton eines dumpfen Donners und Wassergeräusch. Tamino bläst seine Flöte. Sobald sie vom Feuer herauskommen, umarmen sie sich, und bleiben in der Mitte.) [21d]

(The door opens; Tamino and Pamina embrace.)

PAMINA
  My Tamino! Oh, what joy!

TAMINO
  My Pamina! Oh, what joy!
  These are the gates of terror
  that threaten me with danger and death.

PAMINA
  I shall never
  leave your side.
  I myself shall lead you;
  love is my guide!

(She takes his hand.)

  It strews the way with roses,
  for no rose is without a thorn.
  Strike up your magic flute
  so it protects us as we go.
  In a magic hour my father hewed it
  from the deepest roots
  of a thousand-year-old oak
  while thunder and lightning, storm and rain raged.
  Now come and play the flute.
  Let it lead us on our fearful way.

PAMINA and TAMINO, FIRST and SECOND MAN IN
ARMOUR
  By the power of its music we/you walk
  in joy through death's dark night.

*(The doors close after them; Tamino and Pamina are seen walking;
raging fire and howling wind are heard, and at times the sound of
dull thunder and the noise of water. Tamino plays his flute; muffled
timpani provide an intermittent accompaniment. As soon as they
emerge from the fire, they embrace and stand centre stage.)*   [21d]

PAMINA und TAMINO
Wir wandelten durch Feuergluten,
bekämpften mutig die Gefahr.
Dein/mein Ton sei Schutz in Wasserfluten,
so wie er es im Feuer war.

*(Tamino bläst; man sieht sie hinuntersteigen, und nach einiger Zeit
wieder heraufkommen; sogleich öffnet sich eine Türe; man sieht einen
Eingang in einen Tempel, welcher hell beleuchtet ist. Eine feierliche
Stille. Dieser Anblick muss den vollkommensten Glanz darstellen.
Sogleich fällt der Chor unter Trompeten und Pauken ein. Zuvor aber:)*

Ihr Götter, welch ein Augenblick!
Gewähret ist uns Isis' Glück! –

CHOR
Triumph, Triumph! Du edles Paar!
Besieget hast du die Gefahr!
Der Isis Weihe ist nun dein!
Kommt, tretet in den Tempel ein!

(alle ab)

Neunundzwanzigster Auftritt

Das Theater verwandelt sich wieder in den vorigen Garten.

Papageno: später die drei Knaben, Papagena.

PAPAGENO *(pfeift)*
Papagena! Papagena! Papagena!   [21e]
Weibchen! Täubchen! meine Schöne!
Vergebens! Ach! Sie ist verloren!
Ich bin zum Unglück schon geboren.
Ich plauderte, und das war schlecht,
und drum geschieht es mir schon recht!
Seit ich gekostet diesen Wein –
seit ich das schöne Weibchen sah,
so brennt's im Herzenskämmerlein,
so zwicket's hier, so zwicket's da!
Papagena! Herzensweibchen!

PAMINA and TAMINO
    We passed through fiery flames,
    and bravely stood against danger.
    Let your/my music protect us in the waters,
    as it did in the fire.

(Tamino plays; they are seen stepping down, and re-emerging after a while; a door immediately opens, and we see the entrance to a brightly lit temple. A solemn silence. This sight must be utterly radiant. The chorus with trumpets and drums join in, but first:)

    You gods, what a moment!
    The joy of Isis has been granted us.

CHORUS
    Triumph, triumph! You noble couple!
    You have overcome danger!
    You are now blessed by Isis!
    Come, enter the temple!

(All leave.)

Scene 29

The scene changes back to the previous garden.

Papageno, later the Three Boys, Papagena.

PAPAGENO *(calling with his pipes)*
    Papagena! Papagena! Papagena!   [21e]
    Little wife! Little dove! My beauty!
    It's pointless, she's lost!
    I've always been unlucky.
    I blabbed, and that was bad,
    so it serves me right.
    Since I tasted this wine,
    since I saw that lovely little woman,
    my heart has been burning,
    stinging here, stinging there.
    Papagena! Beloved wife!

Papagena, liebes Täubchen!
's ist umsonst! Es ist vergebens!
Müde bin ich meines Lebens!
Sterben macht der Lieb' ein End,
wenn's im Herzen noch so brennt.

(nimmt einen Strick von seiner Mitte)

Diesen Baum da will ich zieren,
mir an ihm den Hals zuschnüren,
weil das Leben mir missfällt;
gute Nacht, du schwarze Welt!
Weil du böse an mir handelst,
mir kein schönes Kind zubandelst,
so ist's aus, so sterbe ich.
Schöne Mädchen, denkt an mich!
Will sich eine um mich Armen,
eh' ich hänge, noch erbarmen,
wohl, so lass ich's diesmal sein!
Rufet nur, ja, oder nein!
Keine hört mich! Alles stille!

(sieht sich um)

Also ist es euer Wille!
Papageno, frisch hinauf,
ende deinen Lebenslauf.

(sieht sich um)

Nun! Ich warte noch. Es sei,
bis man zählet: eins, zwei, drei!

(pfeift)

Eins!

(sieht sich um, pfeift)

Zwei!

(sieht sich um, pfeift)

230

Papagena, sweetheart!
In vain, it's pointless!
I'm tired of my life!
Dying will bring love to an end
if it burns like this in your heart.

(takes a rope from around his waist)

I'm going to adorn this tree here,
and hang myself from it,
since I don't enjoy my life.
Goodnight, grim world!
Since you've been unkind to me
and sent me no pretty girl,
it's all over, I'm going to die:
pretty girls, remember me.
Before I hang, if just one
takes pity on me, poor chap,
I'll let it go this time!
Just shout out, yes or no!
No one hears me, silence everywhere!

(looks round)

So is that what you want?
Papageno, on you go!
End your days.

(looks round)

Well, I'll just wait for a bit!
Until a count of one, two, three!

(plays)

One!

(looks around, plays)

Two!

(looks around, plays)

Drei!

(sieht sich um)

Nun, wohlan! Es bleibt dabei!
Weil mich nichts zurücke hält,
gute Nacht, du falsche Welt!

(will sich hängen)

DIE DREI KNABEN *(fahren herunter)*
Halt ein! O Papageno, und sei klug!
Man lebt nur einmal, dies sei dir genug!

PAPAGENO
Ihr habt gut reden, habt gut scherzen;
doch brennt' es euch, wie mich im Herzen,
ihr würdet auch nach Mädchen gehn.

DIE DREI KNABEN
So lasse deine Glöckchen klingen,
dies wird dein Weibchen zu dir bringen.

PAPAGENO
Ich Narr vergaß der Zauberdinge!

(nimmt sein Instrument heraus)

Erklinge Glockenspiel, erklinge,
ich muss mein liebes Mädchen sehn!

(Die drei Knaben laufen zu ihrem Flugwerk, und bringen Papagena heraus.)

Klinget, Glöckchen, klinget,
schafft mein Mädchen her!
Klinget, Glöckchen, klinget!
Bringt mein Weibchen her!

DIE DREI KNABEN *(fahren auf)*
Nun, Papageno, sieh dich um!

Three!

(looks around)

> Very well, that's how it is,
> since nothing is holding me back,
> good night, you fickle world!

(goes to hang himself)

THE THREE BOYS *(descending)*
> Stop, Papageno! And use your head.
> You have only one life – use it properly.

PAPAGENO
> That's all very well for you to say,
> but if your hearts were burning like mine,
> you'd also go after the girls.

THE THREE BOYS
> Then play your little bells;
> that will lead your little wife to you.

PAPAGENO
> What a fool: I forgot the magic bells.

(takes out his instrument)

> Ring, bells, ring!
> I have to see the girl I love.

(While the bells are playing, the Three Boys run to their flying machine and bring Papagena out.)

> Ring, bells, ring,
> send my girl here!
> Ring, bells, ring,
> bring my little wife here!

THE THREE BOYS *(as they go up)*
> Look behind you, Papageno!

(Papageno sieht sich um; beide haben unter dem Ritornell komisches Spiel.)

PAPAGENO
Pa – Pa – Pa – Pa – Pa – Pa – Papagena!

WEIB
Pa – Pa – Pa – Pa – Pa – Pa – Papageno!

BEIDE
Pa – Pa – Pa – Pa – Pa – Pa – Papagena/Papageno!

PAPAGENO
Bist du mir nun ganz gegeben?

WEIB
Nun bin ich dir ganz gegeben.

PAPAGENO
Nun so sei mein liebes Weibchen!

WEIB
Nun so sei mein Herzenstäubchen!

BEIDE
Welche Freude wird das sein,
wenn die Götter uns bedenken,
unsrer Liebe Kinder schenken,
so liebe kleine Kinderlein!

PAPAGENO
Erst einen kleinen Papageno!

WEIB
Dann eine kleine Papagena!

PAPAGENO
Dann wieder einen Papageno!

WEIB
Dann wieder eine Papagena!

(Papageno looks round; he and Papagena do some comic mime during the ritornello.)

PAPAGENO
Pa – Pa – Pa – Pa – Pa – Pa – Papagena!

WOMAN
Pa – Pa – Pa – Pa – Pa – Pa – Papageno!

BOTH
Pa – Pa – Pa – Pa – Pa – Pa – Papagena/Papageno!

PAPAGENO
Are you all mine now?

PAPAGENA
Now I am all yours.

PAPAGENO
Now be my beloved little wife!

PAPAGENA
Now be my heart's treasure!

BOTH
What a joy it will be
if the gods remember us
and send us lovely children,
lovely little children.

PAPAGENO
First a little Papageno.

PAPAGENA
Then a little Papagena.

PAPAGENO
Then another Papageno.

PAPAGENA
Then another Papagena.

BEIDE

    Papagena! Papageno! Papagena!
    Es ist das höchste der Gefühle,
    wenn viele, viele, viele, viele
    Pa – Pa – Pa – Pa – geno,
    Pa – Pa – Pa – Pa – gena
    Der Eltern Segen werden sein.

(beide ab)

Dreissigster Auftritt

Der Mohr [Monostatos], Königin der Nacht mit allen ihren Damen kommen von beiden Versenkungen; sie tragen schwarze Fackeln in der Hand.

MONOSTATOS

    Nur stille! Stille! Stille! Stille!   [21f]
    Bald dringen wir in Tempel ein!

KÖNIGIN DER NACHT und DIE DREI DAMEN

    Nur stille! Stille! Stille! Stille!
    Bald dringen wir in Tempel ein!

MONOSTATOS

    Doch, Fürstin, halte Wort! Erfülle!
    Dein Kind muss meine Gattin sein!

KÖNIGIN DER NACHT

    Ich halte Wort! Es ist mein Wille,
    mein Kind soll deine Gattin sein!

DIE DREI DAMEN

    Ihr Kind soll deine Gattin sein!

(Man hört dumpfen Donner, Geräusch von Wasser.)

MONOSTATOS

    Doch still, ich höre schrecklich Rauschen,
    wie Donnerton und Wasserfall.

BOTH

> Papagena! Papageno! Papagena!
> There is no greater joy
> than the blessing of many, many, many, many
> Pa – Pa – Pa – Pa – genos,
> Pa – Pa – Pa – Pa – genas
> on their happy parents.

(Both leave.)

Scene 30

The Moor [Monostatos], Queen of the Night and all her Ladies come up through both trapdoors; they are carrying black torches.

MONOSTATOS

> Now quiet, quiet, quiet!   [21f]
> We'll soon break into the Temple.

QUEEN OF THE NIGHT and THE THREE LADIES

> Now quiet, quiet, quiet!
> We'll soon break into the Temple.

MONOSTATOS

> But, Your Highness, keep your word! As you promised,
> your child must be my wife.

QUEEN OF THE NIGHT

> I shall keep my word; it is what I desire.
> My child shall be your wife.

THE THREE LADIES

> Her child shall be your wife.

(Dull thunder is heard, and the sound of rushing water.)

MONOSTATOS

> Hush, I hear a hideous roar
> like thunder and a waterfall.

KÖNIGIN DER NACHT und DIE DREI DAMEN
Ja, fürchterlich ist dieses Rauschen,
wie fernen Donners Wiederhall!

MONASTATOS
Nun sind sie in des Tempels Hallen.

ALLE
Dort wollen wir sie überfallen,
die Frömmler tilgen von der Erd
mit Feuersglut und mächt'gem Schwert!

DIE DREI DAMEN und MONASTATOS *(kniend)*
Dir, große Königin der Nacht,
sei unsrer Rache Opfer gebracht!

(Donner, Blitz, Sturm)

ALLE
Zerschmettert, zernichtet ist unsere Macht,
wir alle gestürzet in ewige Nacht!

(Sie versinken.)

(Sogleich verwandelt sich das ganze Theater in eine Sonne. Sarastro steht erhöht; Tamino, Pamina, beide in priesterlicher Kleidung. Neben ihnen die ägyptischen Priester auf beiden Seiten. Die drei Knaben halten Blumen.)

SARASTRO
Die Strahlen der Sonne vertreiben die Nacht,
zernichten der Heuchler erschlichene Macht!

CHOR
Heil sei euch Geweihten!   [21g1]
Ihr dranget durch Nacht!
Dank sei dir, Osiris,
dank dir, Isis, gebracht!
Es siegte die Stärke   [21g2]
und krönet zum Lohn
die Schönheit und Weisheit   [21g3]
mit ewiger Kron'!

238

QUEEN OF THE NIGHT and THE THREE LADIES
Yes, this roar is fearful,
like the echo of distant thunder.

MONOSTATOS
They are now in the Temple halls.

ALL
There we shall overwhelm them.
With burning fire and mighty sword
we shall rid the world of these bigots!

THE THREE LADIES and MONOSTATOS *(kneeling)*
To you, great Queen of the Night,
we dedicate our vengeance!

(thunder, lightning, storm)

ALL
Our power is shattered and destroyed,
we are plunged into everlasting night!

(They sink down.)

(The whole scene immediately turns into a sun. Sarastro is seen in an elevated position; Tamino and Pamina in priestly robes. Next to them, on both sides, the Egyptian priests. The Three Boys are holding flowers.)

SARASTRO
The rays of the sun drive the night away,
and destroy the impostors' devious power.

CHORUS
Hail to you, Initiates!   [21g1]
You have broken through the darkness!
Thanks be to you, Osiris,
to you, Isis, thanks be given!
Courage triumphed,   [21g2]
and beauty and wisdom
are rewarded   [21g3]
with an everlasting crown!

Select Discography

There is no up-to-date survey in English of the opera on disc. The website https://operadis-opera-discography.org.uk/CLMOZAUB.HTM lists full details of 103 complete audio performances of *Die Zauberflöte*, including transfers of many 'off-the-air' broadcasts, up until 2009. For discussions of selected recordings up to 1979, see Peter Branscombe, *'Die Zauberflöte'*, *Opera on Record*, ed. Alan Blyth (London: Hutchinson, 1979), pp. 106–18 and, up to 1993, Roland Graeme, *'Die Zauberflöte'*, *The Metropolitan Opera Guide to Recorded Opera*, ed. Paul Gruber (London and New York: Thames and Hudson, 1993), pp. 332–44.

This selection highlights some of the leading interpretations. None of the recordings below includes the complete dialogue as it appears in the Neue Mozart-Ausgabe, but some indication is given in the following list as to which have no dialogue, have the dialogue spoken by actors or incorporate other features.

YEAR	CAST	CONDUCTOR/ORCHESTRA/ CHORUS	LABEL
	Pamina		
	Tamino		
	Papageno		
	Queen of the Night		
	Sarastro		
	Monostatos		
	Speaker		
	Papagena		

1937*	Jarmila Novotná Helge Rosvaenge Willi Domgraf- Fassbaender Júlia Osváth Alexander Kipnis William Wernigk Alfred Jerger Dora Komarek	Arturo Toscanini Vienna Philharmonic Vienna State Opera Chorus	Naxos/ Pristine Audio (live) Minimal dialogue
1937/ 38*	Tiana Lemnitz Helge Rosvaenge Gerhard Hüsch Erna Berger Wilhelm Strienz Heinrich Tessmer Walter Großmann Irma Beilke	Thomas Beecham Berlin Philharmonic Waldo Favre Choir	Naxos No dialogue
1950*	Imgard Seefried Anton Dermota Erich Kunz Wilma Lipp Ludwig Weber Peter Klein George London Emmy Loose	Herbert von Karajan Vienna Philharmonic Vienna Singverein	Warner Classics No dialogue
1951*	Imgard Seefried Anton Dermota Erich Kunz Wilma Lipp Josef Greindl Peter Klein Paul Schöffler Edith Oravez	Wilhelm Furtwängler Vienna Philharmonic Vienna State Opera Chorus	Naxos Historical (live)
1955*	Maria Stader Ernst Häfliger Dietrich Fischer-Dieskau Rita Streich Josef Greindl	Ferenc Fricsay Berlin RIAS Symphony Orchestra and Chamber Choir	DG Dialogue abridged and all except Fischer-Dieskau's spoken by actors

Martin Vantin
Kim Borg
Lisa Otto

1962	Joan Carlyle	Otto Klemperer	Testament
	Richard Lewis		(live)
	Geraint Evans	Royal Opera House	
	Joan Sutherland	Orchestra and Chorus	
	David Kelly		
	Robert Bowman		
	Hans Hotter		
	Jenifer Eddy		
1964	Gundula Janowitz	Otto Klemperer	Warner
	Nicolai Gedda		Classics
	Walter Berry	Philharmonia	
	Lucia Popp	Orchestra and	No dialogue
	Gottlob Frick	Chorus	
	Gerhard Unger		
	Franz Crass		
	Ruth-Margret Pütz		
1964	Evelyn Lear	Karl Böhm	DG
	Fritz Wunderlich		
	Dietrich Fischer-Dieskau	Berlin Philharmonic	Dialogue
	Roberta Peters		abridged
	Franz Crass	Berlin RIAS	
	Friedrich Lenz	Chamber Choir	
	Hans Hotter		
	Lisa Otto		
1969	Pilar Lorengar	Georg Solti	Decca
	Stuart Burrows		
	Hermann Prey	Vienna Philharmonic	(includes
	Cristina Deutekom		sound
	Martti Talvela	Vienna State Opera Chorus	effects)
	Gerhard Stolze		
	Dietrich Fischer-Dieskau		
	Renate Holm		

1972	Anneliese Rothenberger Peter Schreier Walter Berry Edda Moser Kurt Moll Willi Brokmeier Theo Adam Olivera Miljakovič	Wolfgang Sawallisch Bavarian State Opera and Chorus	Warner Classics (includes the disputed 'Pamina, wo bist du?' Act Two duet for Tamino and Pamina, which Schikaneder inserted for the 1802 Theater an der Wien revival and claimed to have been written by Mozart)
1978	Kiri Te Kanawa Peter Hoffmann Philippe Huttenlocher Edita Gruberova Kurt Moll Norbert Orth José van Dam Kathleen Battle	Alain Lombard Strasbourg Philharmonic Opéra du Rhin Chorus	Erato
1980	Edith Mathis Francisco Araiza Gottfried Hornik Karin Ott José van Dam Heinz Kruse Claudio Nicolai Janet Perry	Herbert von Karajan Berlin Philharmonic Deutsche Oper Chorus	DG
1980	Ileana Cotrubas Eric Tappy Christian Boesch Zdisława Donat Martti Talvela Horst Hiestermann José van Dam Elizabeth Kales	James Levine Vienna Philharmonic Vienna State Opera Chorus	Sony Papageno's dialogue includes some Viennese dialect
1981	Lucia Popp Siegfried Jerusalem Wolfgang Brendel Edita Gruberová	Bernard Haitink Bavarian Radio Symphony and Chorus	Warner Classics (includes sound effects)

Roland Bracht
Heinz Zednik
Norman Bailey
Brigitte Linder

1984	Margaret Price	Colin Davis	Philips
	Peter Schreier		
	Mikael Melbye	Dresden State	Dialogue
	Luciana Serra	Orchestra	spoken
	Kurt Moll		by actors
	Robert Tear	Leipzig Radio	
	Theo Adam	Chorus	
	Maria Venuti		
1987	Barbara Bonney	Nikolaus	Teldec
	Hans Peter Blochwitz	Harnoncourt	
	Anton Scharinger		Dialogue
	Edita Gruberová	Zurich Opera	mostly
	Matti Salminen	Orchestra and	replaced by
	Peter Keller	Chorus	a spoken
	Thomas Hampson		narration
	Edith Schmid		
1989	Kiri Te Kanawa	Neville Marriner	Philips
	Francisco Araiza		
	Olaf Bär	Academy of	
	Cheryl Studer	St Martin in the	
	Samuel Ramey	Fields	
	Aldo Baldin		
	José van Dam	Ambrosian Chorus	
	Eva Lind		
1990	Ruth Ziesak	Georg Solti	Decca
	Uwe Heilmann		
	Michael Kraus	Vienna Philharmonic	(includes some
	Sumi Jo		sound effects)
	Kurt Moll	Vienna State Opera	
	Heinz Zednik	Chorus	
	Andreas Schmidt		
	Lotte Leitner		

1990	Dawn Upshaw Anthony Rolfe Johnson	Roger Norrington	Erato
	Andreas Schmidt Beverly Hoch Cornelius Hauptmann	London Classical Players	(includes some sound effects)
	Guy de Mey Olaf Bär Catherine Pierard	Schütz Choir of London	
1991	Barbara Hendricks Jerry Hadley	Charles Mackerras	Telarc
	Thomas Allen June Anderson Robert Lloyd Helmut Wildhaber Gottfried Hornik Ulrike Steinsky	Scottish Chamber Orchestra and Chorus	(includes 'Pamina, wo bist du?'Act Two duet)
1996	Rosa Mannion Hans Peter Blochwitz	William Christie	Erato
	Anton Scharinger Natalie Dessay Reinhard Hagen Steven Cole Willard White Linda Kitchen	Les Arts Florissants Orchestra and Chorus	Dialogue spoken by actors
1996	Christiane Oelze Michael Schade	John Eliot Gardiner	DG Archiv
	Gerald Finley Cyndia Sieden Harry Peeters	English Baroque Soloists	
	Uwe Peper Detlef Roth Constanze Backes	Monteverdi Choir	
2005	Rebecca Evans Barry Banks	Charles Mackerras	Chandos
	Simon Keenlyside Elizabeth Vidal	London Philharmonic	(in English)
	John Tomlinson	Geoffrey Mitchell Choir	

	John Graham Hall		
	Christopher Purves		
	Lesley Garrett		
2006	Dorothea Röschmann	Claudio Abbado	DG
	Christoph Strehl		
	Hanno Müller-Brachmann	Mahler Chamber Orchestra	
	Erika Miklósa		
	René Pape	Arnold Schoenberg Choir	
	Kurt Azesberger		
	Georg Zeppenfeld		
	Julia Kleiter		
2010	Marlis Petersen	René Jacobs	Harmonia Mundi
	Daniel Behle		
	Daniel Schmutzhard	Akademie für Alte Musik Berlin	(includes sound effects and the fullest dialogue yet recorded)
	Anna-Kristiina Kaappola		
	Marcos Fink		
	Kurt Azesberger	RIAS Chamber Choir	
	Konstantin Wolff		
	Sunhae Im		

* mono

Die Zauberflöte on DVD

There is no up-to-date survey in English of the opera on DVD. The website https://operadis-opera-discography.org.uk/CLMOZAUB.HTM lists full details of 27 DVD or VHS recordings of *Die Zauberflöte* up until 2009. An annotated list up to 2003 – including early and related films, both commercially released and otherwise – may be found in Ken Wlaschin, *Encyclopedia of Opera on Screen* (Yale 2004), pp. 779–83.

This selection highlights some of the leading interpretations.

YEAR	CAST	CONDUCTOR/ORCHESTRA/	DIRECTOR/
	Pamina	CHORUS	COMPANY/
	Tamino		LABEL
	Papageno		
	Queen of the Night		
	Sarastro		
	Monostatos		
	Speaker		
	Papagena		
1975	Irma Urrila	Eric Ericson	Ingmar
	Josef Köstlinger		Bergman
	Håkan Hagegård	Swedish Radio	
	Birgit Nordin	Orchestra and	Feature film
	Ulrik Cold	Chorus	
	Ragnar Ulfung		(in Swedish)
	Erik Saedén		
	Elizabeth Erikson		Criterion

Year	Cast	Conductor / Orchestra	Director / Production
1978	Felicity Lott Leo Goeke Benjamin Luxon May Sandoz Thomas Thomaschke Willard White John Fryatt Elisabeth Conquet	Bernard Haitink London Philharmonic Glyndebourne Chorus	John Cox (designed by David Hockney) Glyndebourne Festival Arthaus Musik
1982	Ileana Cotrubas Peter Schreier Christian Boesch Edita Gruberová Martti Talvela Horst Hiestermann Walter Berry Gudrun Sieber	James Levine Vienna Philharmonic Vienna State Opera Chorus	Jean-Pierre Ponnelle Salzburg Festival TDK
1983	Lucia Popp Francisco Araiza Wolfgang Brendel Edita Gruberová Kurt Rydl Norbert Orth Jan-Hendrik Rootering Gudrun Sieber	Wolfgang Sawallisch Bavarian State Opera Orchestra and Chorus	August Everding Bavarian State Opera Philips
1989	Ann Christine Biel Stefan Dahlberg Mikael Samuelson Birgit Louise Frandsen László Polgár Magnus Kyhle Petteri Salomaa Birgitta Larsson	Arnold Östman Drottningholm Theatre Orchestra and Chorus	Göran Järvefelt Drottningholm Court Theatre Arthaus Musik
1992	Ulrike Sonntag Deon van der Walt Thomas Mohr Andrea Frei Cornelius Hauptmann Kevin Connors Sebastian Holecek Patricia Rozario	Wolfgang Gönnenwein Ludwigsburg Festival Orchestra and Chorus	Axel Manthey Ludwigsburg Festival Arthaus Musik

2000	Malin Hartelius Piotr Beczala Anton Scharinger Elena Moşuc Matti Salminen Volker Vogel Jacob Will Julia Neumann	Franz Welser-Möst Zurich Opera Orchestra and Chorus	Jonathan Miller Zurich Opera TDK
2000	Dorothea Röschmann Piotr Beczala Detlef Roth Désirée Rancatore Matti Salminen Uwe Peper Wolfgang Schöne Gaële Le Roi	Iván Fischer Opéra National de Paris Orchestra and Chorus	Benno Besson Opéra National de Paris Arthaus Musik
2003	Dorothea Röschmann Will Hartmann Simon Keenlyside Diana Damrau Franz-Josef Selig Adrian Thompson Thomas Allen Ailish Tynan	Colin Davis Royal Opera House Orchestra and Chorus	David McVicar Royal Opera House Opus Arte
2006	Amy Carson Joseph Kaiser Benjamin Jay Davis Lyubov Petrova René Pape Tom Randle Ben Uttley Silvia Moi	James Conlon Chamber Orchestra of Europe and Chorus	Kenneth Branagh Feature film (in English) Revolver
2006	Genia Kühmeier Paul Groves Christian Gerhaher Diana Damrau René Pape Bürkhard Ulrich Franz Grundheber Irena Bespalovaite	Riccardo Muti Vienna Philharmonic Vienna State Opera Chorus	Pierre Audi Salzburg Festival Decca

2007	Julia Kleiter Christoph Strehl Ruben Drole Elena Moşuc Matti Salminen Rudolf Schasching Gabriel Bermudez Eva Liebau	Nikolaus Harnoncourt Zurich Opera Orchestra and Chorus	Martin Kušej Zurich Opera DG
2011	Genia Kühmeier Saimir Pirgu Alex Esposito Albina Shagimuratova Günther Groissböck Peter Bronder Roman Sadnik Ailish Tynan	Roland Böer La Scala Orchestra and La Scala Academy Chorus	William Kentridge La Scala Opus Arte
2013	Kate Royal Pavol Breslik Michael Nagy Ana Durlovski Dimitry Ivashchenko James Elliott José van Dam Regula Mühlemann	Simon Rattle Berlin Philharmonic Berlin Radio Chorus	Baden-Baden Easter Festival (concert version) Berliner Philharmoniker
2015	Christina Landshamer Maximilian Schmitt Thomas Oliemans Íride Martínez Brindley Sherratt Wolfgang Ablinger- Sperrhacke Detlef Roth Nina Lejderman	Marc Albrecht Netherlands Chamber Orchestra Dutch National Opera Chorus	Simon McBurney De Nederlandse Opera Opus Arte

Select Bibliography

Abert, Hermann, *W.A. Mozart*, trans. Stewart Spencer (New Haven, CT: Yale University Press, 2007)

Angermüller, Rudolph, *Mozart's Operas*, trans. Stewart Spencer (New York, NY: Rizzoli International, 1988)

Branscombe, Peter, *W.A. Mozart: 'Die Zauberflöte'* (Cambridge: Cambridge University Press, 1991)

Brophy, Brigid, *Mozart the Dramatist: A New View of Mozart, His Operas and His Age*, revised edn. (London: Libris, 1988)

Cairns, David, *Mozart and His Operas* (London: Allen Lane, 2006)

Dent, E.J., *Mozart's Operas: A Critical Study*, 2nd edn. (Oxford: Oxford University Press, 1947)

Einstein, Alfred, *Mozart, His Character, His Work*, trans. Arthur Mendel and Nathan Broder (London: Cassell, 1946)

Eisen, Cliff and Keefe, Simon P. (eds.), *The Cambridge Mozart Encyclopedia* (Cambridge: Cambridge University Press, 2006)

Eisen, Cliff (ed.), *Mozart: A Life in Letters*, trans. Stewart Spencer (London: Penguin, 2006)

Gutman, Robert W., *Mozart: A Cultural Biography* (New York, NY: Harcourt Brace & Co., 1999)

Heartz, Daniel (ed.), *Mozart's Operas* (Berkeley, CA: University of California Press, 1990)

Hunter, Mary, *Mozart's Operas: A Companion* (New Haven, CT: Yale University Press, 2008)

Keefe, Simon P. (ed.), *The Cambridge Companion to Mozart* (Cambridge: Cambridge University Press, 2003)

Keefe, Simon P., *Mozart in Vienna: The Final Decade* (Cambridge: Cambridge University Press, 2017)

Keefe, Simon P. (ed.), *Mozart in Context* (Cambridge: Cambridge University Press, 2018)

Kerman, Joseph, *Opera as Drama* (New York, NY: Alfred Knopf, 1956, rev. 2005)

Landon, H.C. Robbins, *1791: Mozart's Last Year* (London: Thames and Hudson, 1988)

Landon, H.C. Robbins, *Mozart, the Golden Years 1781–1791* (London: Thames and Hudson, 1989)

Landon, H.C. Robbins (ed.), *The Mozart Compendium* (London: Thames and Hudson, 1990)

Landon, H.C. Robbins and Mitchell, Donald (eds.), *The Mozart Companion* (London: Rockliff, 1956)

Mann, William, *The Operas of Mozart* (London: Cassell, 1977)

Moberly, R.B., *Three Mozart Operas* (London: Dodd Mead, 1967)

Rushton, Julian, *The New Grove Guide to Mozart and His Operas* (New York: Oxford University Press, 2007)

Sadie, Stanley (ed.), *Wolfgang Amadè Mozart* (Oxford: Clarendon Press, 1996)

Till, Nicholas, *Mozart and the Enlightenment: Truth, Virtue and Beauty in Mozart's Operas* (London: Faber and Faber, 1992)

Woodfield, Ian, *Performing Operas for Mozart: Impresarios, Singers and Troupes* (Cambridge: Cambridge University Press, 2017)

Mozart Websites*

In English or with an English-language option

Bärenreiter Mozart Portal   *www.mozart-portal.de*

International Mozart Foundation   *www.mozarteum.at*

The Mozart Project   *www.mozartproject.org/index.html*

Mozart's Musical Diary (British Library Online Gallery):
                    www.bl.uk/onlinegallery/ttp/ttpbooks.html

Neue Mozart-Ausgabe Online   *www.nma.at*

OperaGlass Mozart   *opera.stanford.edu/Mozart*

* Links valid at the time of publication in 2019.

Note on the Contributors

Kenneth Chalmers is a translator and writer on music. He has translated numerous opera libretti and is Head of Surtitles at the Royal Opera House. His translations include the final volume of Lorenzo Bianconi and Giorgio Pestelli's *The History of Italian Opera* (Chicago University Press, 2004) and Constantin Floros's *New Ears for New Music* (Peter Lang, 2014).

Julian Rushton is Emeritus Professor of Music at the University of Leeds. He has published extensively on Mozart, including *The New Grove Guide to Mozart and His Operas* (Oxford University Press, 2007) and Cambridge Opera Handbooks to *Don Giovanni* and *Idomeneo* (Cambridge University Press, 1981 and 1993).

Hugo Shirley is a musicologist and critic based in Berlin. He was editor of *30-Second Opera* (Ivy Press, 2015) and is a regular contributor to *Gramophone* and *Opera*. He writes widely on opera and classical music and has published in the *Cambridge Opera Journal* and the *Journal of the Royal Musical Association*.

Nicholas Till is a historian of opera and music theatre, and Professor of Opera and Music Theatre at the University of Sussex. He is the author of *Mozart and the Enlightenment* (Faber and Faber, 1992), and editor of *The Cambridge Companion to Opera Studies* (Cambridge University Press, 2012) and *Beckett and Musicality* (Routledge, 2014). His current research is on early opera and modernity.

Acknowledgements

We would like to thank John Allison of *Opera*, Mike Markiewicz of ArenaPAL, Charles Johnston, Mike Ashman and also Christoph Großpietsch of the Internationale Stiftung Mozarteum, Salzburg, for their assistance and advice in the preparation of this guide.

www.overturepublishing.com
www.eno.org